INTO THE VALLEY *of* SHADOW

Into the Valley of Shadow

Dennis Thurman,
with Kelly Thurman Phillips

Xulon Press
2301 Lucien Way #415
Maitland, FL 32751
407.339.4217
www.xulonpress.com

© 2019 by Dennis Thurman, with Kelly Thurman Phillips

All rights reserved solely by the author. The author guarantees all contents are original and do not infringe upon the legal rights of any other person or work. No part of this book may be reproduced in any form without the permission of the author. The views expressed in this book are not necessarily those of the publisher.

Unless otherwise indicated, Scripture quotations taken from the New King James Version (NKJV). Copyright © 1982 by Thomas Nelson, Inc. Used by permission. All rights reserved.

Printed in the United States of America.

ISBN-13: 978-1-54567-813-8

TABLE OF CONTENTS

→→→→ ❃ ←←←←

FOREWORD, by Dr. Johnny Hunt vii

ENDORSEMENTS ix

ACKNOWLEDGMENTS xv

INTRODUCTION xvii

Chapter 1:   INTO THE VALLEY OF SHADOW—
  The Journey Begins 1

Chapter 2:   BEING THANKFUL 5

Chapter 3:   PURPOSE IN OUR PAIN 8

Chapter 4:   GOD LEADS US ALONG 14

Chapter 5:   HERE'S HOPE! 18

Chapter 6:   AN ATTITUDE OF GRATITUDE 23

Chapter 7:   OUR KEEPER 31

Chapter 8:   ABOVE THE STORM CLOUDS 36

Chapter 9:   WHEN THE RUG IS JERKED
  OUT FROM UNDER YOU 40

Chapter 10: UPS AND DOWNS—
      The Elevator of Cancer Treatment 45

Chapter 11: BIRTHDAY IN A HOSPITAL BED. 51

Chapter 12: BETTER AND BRIGHTER DAYS 57

Chapter 13: DESCENT INTO DARKNESS 65

Chapter 14: FINAL DAYS. 72

Chapter 15: UNCLE CALEB. 77

Chapter 16: MIGHTY MYA—A Celebration of Her Life 81

Chapter 17: A GRIEF OBTAINED 94

Chapter 18: A BIRTHDAY POEM AND DRAWINGS
      IN CHALK. 99

Chapter 19: WHY?. 101

Chapter 20: MORE MEMORIES. 118

CONCLUSION—from Mya's Mother Kelly:
      Moving Forward. 127

Foreword

→→→→ ❋ ←←←←

Have you ever picked up a book to read the introduction—only to find out you could not put it down? That is exactly what happened to me when I picked up "Into the Valley of Shadow." This is a story of something that you pray will never happen to you. It is something that is so unnatural—and that is a mother and a father having the sad duty of watching their precious child suffer, and then later exit this world to be at home with the Lord. This is what I would call a real story, not spiritualized, but a devoted journey, a journey of transition of different feelings, of lessons learned, of influence shared and I could go on and on.

Have you ever wondered how you can give thanks for things that are so difficult to live with on a day-to-day basis? No one would say it is easy, but Kelly has been there, and she has come out on the other side. She is so quick to give credit to the one who gave her strength to make it day by day. All of us have people in our life or our own personal experiences that has caused us to ask questions that there seems to be no earthly answer for. Be encouraged, there is one who speaks of life and death that knows victory in both. He and He alone is the one that gives hope where there seems to be no hope. It has been said that we can go forty days without eating, four days without water, four minutes without oxygen, but it seems that we cannot survive four seconds without hope. "Into the Valley of Shadow" is a book of hope. It is a book of survival, a book of how to make it when there seems to be no obvious path to tread—no GPS that can point you in the right direction. Yet, day by day, there is one that takes our hand, sustains and encourages us, as we walk through the valley. I believe you will agree with me, in that this book is difficult to put down. You find yourself anticipating the next day—wondering can one really make it. The question is constantly on our lips, "How will they make it another day?" Then, only to travel with them, as an unseen presence who makes Himself so physically real as truth speaks life, encouragement, and hope.

It has been said that every life that touches another has influence. Little Mya Grace will influence you as she has influenced me. God used her to supernaturally touch her mom, her dad, her grandfather in particular, her uncle and all that came in contact with her. One of the newest songs says it all, "Hope has a name and it's Jesus." Jesus is clearly seen—caring, showing compassion, lifting, and loving on days where the next step almost seems impossible.

Thank you, Kelly, and thank you Dennis for the bravery of your soul to pen such a journey. My life has been enriched already. I can hardly wait to see the stories that will abound from these pages.

Johnny Hunt
Senior Pastor First Baptist Church Woodstock, Georgia
Senior Vice President, North American Mission Board Evangelism and Pastoral Leadership
Former President Southern Baptist Convention

Endorsements

"Into the Valley of Shadow" by Brother Dennis Thurman will be a great blessing to you. It is a story of great sorrow, yet triumphant faith. God's people will be taught and encouraged by this remarkable account.

> Jerry Vines, Two time President of the Southern Baptist Convention; Pastor Emeritus, First Baptist Church, Jacksonville, Florida

Into the Valley of Shadow is a book that goes straight to the heart! This book conveys the most heartfelt, honest, and hopeful story about earthly loss and future heavenly reunion that I have ever read. Every person who reads this book will gain a powerful perspective that will help them navigate the dark valleys that we all must face. This is must reading for everyone who needs to see God in the midst of the greatest disappointments in life.

> David Horton
> President, Fruitland Baptist Bible College

Into The Valley of Shadow

Nothing affects us so profoundly, as the difficult times in our lives, when the people we love face sickness and death. It is in these times that we look for answers and comfort, as we try to deal with our loss, but it is also a time when our faith helps us deal with the unimaginable pain. I was privileged to know Dennis during such a time, and to see him minister and be ministered to. I know you will be touched by his words and advice. His faithful words are a worthwhile investment for any family.

NC Congressman Mark Meadows

Into the Valley of Shadow bids the reader to walk with its author, a well-loved pastor, through his young granddaughter's painful struggle with cancer, her parents' desperate and heroic response, and the darkness of grief which threatened their family's faith in an all-loving God, and left them with questions only He can answer. Dennis captures our attention with his excellent writing and our hearts with his transparency. Kelly, Mya's mother, shares her journal entries of hope and despair, of love which lasts beyond the grave into life everlasting. I recommend this love story to anyone who needs a hand to hold through the valley of shadow, and as insight to young ministers who perhaps are not acquainted with grief.

Karen Holcomb, author/illustrator Proverbial Kids©
MA Communications, Southwestern Seminary

Endorsements

Many people have asked, "Where is God in the midst of my suffering?," concluding that He was nowhere to be found. However, Pastor Dennis Thurman and his daughter, Kelly Thurman Phillips, have out of their own painful, personal suffering penned a riveting testimony of how they found God's ever-presence in both His Word and the miracles He performed during the agonizing death of his granddaughter and her daughter, Mighty Mya Grace Phillips. This book is more than a grief observed, it is a grief obtained that produced in them a deeper faith in God and love among family members. This book has blessed my heart and it will bless yours, too.

Matt Queen
Associate Professor and L. R. Scarborough Chair of Evangelism ("The Chair of Fire")
Associate Dean of the Roy Fish School of Evangelism and Missions, Southwestern Baptist Theological Seminary, Fort Worth, Texas

This book is a great resource for helping individuals live in the light of God's presence when a loved one is dealing with a serious illness. It gives the reader an opportunity to observe how a family whose lives are deeply rooted in Christ is able to navigate through one of the most difficult life situations. Into the Valley of the Shadow introduces you to a wonderful, charming seven year old girl name, Mya Grace, who was stricken with a vicious form of cancer that eventually claimed her physical life, but it could not destroy her eternal life in Christ. This is her family's story, primarily told by Mya's grandfather pastor and her mother.

It will cause you to weep as you identify with her family's pain and longing for Mya to receive physical healing, but you will also be amazed when you discover how they were still able to rejoice in God during that difficult experience because of their assurance that a loving, compassionate God was always in control of their situation. You will be challenged as you recognize the depth of this family's trust in God and also the spiritual faith of a precious little girl who focused more on those around her than her own sickness and gave her best in the fight for her life.

Milton A. Hollifield Jr.
Executive Director-Treasurer of the Baptist State
Convention of North Carolina

I have never had the privilege of meeting Dennis Thurman in person, though I consider him a trusted mentor of mine through social media. My wife and I have traveled "into the valley of shadow" before with two miscarriages and two failed adoptions, and have felt a kindred spirit with the Thurman family since first hearing the story of sweet Mya. The heartache is unimaginable, but Dennis writes in such a way to turn the heartache into hope, giving the reader a glimpse at the presence of God amid trials that tempt us to despair. Oh, to be a fly on the wall to watch the reunion of Dennis and Mya in Glory! Until then, I believe Into the Valley of Shadow will take the reader on a journey worth taking. It's a journey of hope, a journey of truth, and a journey worth every word, every page, and every chapter.

Endorsements

Matt Henslee
Pastor of Mayhill Baptist Church, Mayhill, New Mexico,
and co-author of *Replanting Rural Churches:
God's Plan and Call in the Middle of Nowhere*

Mya Grace Phillips, a little girl who bravely battled cancer, will deepen your faith and serve as a powerful reminder of the promises we have in Jesus. Mya's life is a must read testimony of how God "works all things together for good" even in the midst of suffering. "Into the Valley of Shadow" is a beautiful real-life story that will encourage and inspire any reader!

David Sims
Senior Pastor, Richland Creek Community Church

Honesty is a value we hold in high regard, but are fain to practice it in tough times. It is hard to be honest when everything in our world seems to be pressing against us, forcing the collapse of our preferences for those we love. In the painful search for answers, some shroud their experience with trite sayings or hollow clichés. Dennis Thurman and his family did not! The transparency and honesty of their struggles are recorded on these pages for all to see. They expressed what many followers of Christ are reluctant to say. Their story is real. Their struggles with grief and the realities of a fallen world are heart-wrenching. They ask honest questions and expose their deepest struggles. All who read this story will be stronger for life's next battles.

K. Allan Blume
Retired pastor, former editor of the Biblical Recorder

Christian grief and hope can only truly be written from the perspective singularly possessed by persons who have walked through the valley of the shadow of death. Pastor Dennis Thurman and his daughter, Kelly, share a poignant glimpse of the struggles they experienced during the sickness and homegoing of precious Mya. They reveal the ragged reality of the process, the path, the pain and the ultimate promise of hope that only the Lord Jesus can provide. Strengthened by the Holy Spirit, Scripture, songs of praise and prayer, they bear witness to the sufficiency of His grace in our darkest hours. This powerful book will move your heart to tears of grief and joyous hope, encourage your trust in our Lord and draw you closer to our Shepherd.

Don L. McCutcheon, Sr., D.Min.
Former State Director of Evangelism for the Baptist State Convention of North Carolina

Acknowledgments

I am thankful for my wife, Marilyn, who has been by my side in the ups and downs of ministry for over four decades. She has been the most significant person in my spiritual development—a model of devotion to the Lord, her husband, and family.

I am grateful for my daughter, Kelly, who along with her husband Logan, still hurt, yet live in hope of the resurrection. They have ministered to so many hurting people out of the depths of their own experience of great grief and greater grace. Kelly's diary of this walk through the valley of shadow is woven into the fabric of this book. Her siblings, Chris and Caleb, contributed touching tributes in this text. While her sister, Kascy, did not write anything, her support of her sister was more profound than anything she might say.

I am most thankful to God who blessed us with Mya Grace—the large faith in a little girl, and her smile that could brighten the darkest days. Because of Christ's victory over the grave, we anticipate a glad reunion day with her!

A special word of appreciation goes to Jessica Burch, who edited this manuscript and made several helpful suggestions.

Soli Deo Gloria!

Introduction

What a joy Mya Grace brought into our lives—indeed, to everyone who crossed her path. There was a radiance about her—a delightful pixie, who danced across the theater of our life. The thought never darkened our minds that the drama would become a tragedy—that this beautiful flower would too soon wither under the killing frost of cancer.

The optimism we felt is seen in the dedication letter Mya's mom, Kelly, wrote to her. Our church had prepared a treasure box for her—as we did for all the children—and on the day Mya would be dedicated to the Lord, letters were to be placed inside, as well as other keepsakes, to be opened by Mya on her thirteenth birthday. Here is what Kelly penned:

> Dear Mya,
>
> I never realized how much I could love a little girl until you came along! You have been the perfect addition to our family. Your dad and I are so blessed to have you in our lives. God always knows what is

best, but when He chose to surprise us with you, I had no idea how much joy was waiting for us! You are such a beautiful baby girl. It melts my heart to look at you, especially when you are smiling with that big, beaming smile! Your little eyes almost close when you smile at us and your face shines. You have a way of lighting up a room! There is so much love and laughter with you in our lives. I am so glad you are mine.

Just like with your brother Isaiah, we knew when you were born that you were a miracle and a gift from God. We also knew that we wanted to thank Him for you and acknowledge that you are ours only because of Him. So, we stood before our church, along with many other parents and their babies, and publicly dedicated you back to the Lord (you were born in a baby booming year for our church — twenty+ babies!). We are trusting Him to guide you and to guard your heart, soul, mind and body. Our prayer for you sweet girl, is that you will love the Lord your God with all your heart, soul, mind and strength. I pray for your salvation to come early and while you are young so that you will have that open communication with God throughout your whole life. You can always come to me with anything, but even more importantly, God is there for you. Talk to Him and study His word. I tell you all the time that you are my beautiful princess and to me, you are.

But you can really be a princess one day when you become a child of the King. I am not a perfect mom. I have already failed you and I will unfortunately do it again, but I will try to do my best. I am sorry for my imperfections and for ever letting you down, and I hope that you will always forgive me. But He is a perfect father and is always ready and eager to listen, no matter how big or small your problem seems to you. He will never disappoint you!

I am looking forward to spending life with you! You are already growing up so fast and sometimes I wish I could just stop time. I would love to be able to hold you and care for you forever, but I know I cannot. I am so thankful for a Heavenly father who will though. You can never outgrow His arms. As hard as it is already, and will be even harder in the future, I will try my best to trust Him to take care of you. He can do a better job than I can! I am excited to see what the future holds for our family. I look forward to becoming your best friend. Hopefully you will like to go shopping! I know there are so many special memories that are waiting for us. I just cannot thank God enough for bringing this bundle of joy, Mya Grace, into my life. I will love you forever sweet girl!

Love always,
Mommy

So, as her Papa Pastor, I would call Logan and Kelly to give Mya back to God who gave her to them. We prayed and dedicated her to the Lord. Sure enough, she would later make a profession of faith, and I had the privilege of baptizing her. She was given to God, and God took her. She would never get to open her treasure box, for God opened His gates to His treasure chamber and set her as a sparkling jewel in heaven.

Mighty Mya—that was the nickname given to Mya Grace Phillips. It had nothing to do with her stature—she was a petite little girl—but was a tribute to her courage and determination. In a battle with extremely aggressive cancer, she faced her foe with incredible bravery. The torturous treatments, which took her hair and made her nauseous, tested her, but did not triumph over her. The prolonged stays, isolated in a hospital, when other children were free to run and play with her friends, did not overcome her. Mya was a champion. That power came from her faith—the simple, childlike faith in Jesus whom she loved. Even in her lowest days, she would often be heard singing praises to the Lord. We witnessed a community come together to pray for and support Mighty Mya. Her name became known far and wide. Her story was read and spread by tens of thousands. The love of her family and friends helped fuel her passion to conquer the horrible disease. Mya Grace inspired us to be more committed to the eternal, more caring for others, and more courageous in the challenges we all will face. On July 14, 2016, Mya beat cancer forever. She went home to be with Jesus, and her powerful legacy lives on. Now, we follow in her tiny footprints, and look forward to seeing her again in that wonderful Gloryland!

This is her story. As we travel through those tortuous months, you will find posts that were written from Mya's mother, Kelly.

Introduction

These chronological journal entries will be interspersed with my commentary. Additionally, during this time, I was writing a number of blog posts and devotional thoughts that were meant to encourage those who were praying for and supporting us in those difficult days. Expressing those Biblical messages also was therapeutic to me. I am praying that as you read this book it will be a blessing to you. May God take this awful pain and use it for amazing purposes—for His glory and your good. Walk with us into the valley of shadow. Eventually, we will all make that trip, and we trust God will use our journey to prepare you for yours.

Chapter 1

INTO THE VALLEY OF SHADOW—
The Journey Begins

I can recall it like it was yesterday. That unutterable word rising from the deepest pit of dread—which, though we knew was a possibility—we had tried to push into the margins of our minds. The word—cancer—the horror of human afflictions. The doctor's diagnosis fell like a sledgehammer on my baby daughter, driving her to the floor in a puddle of tears.

I had been at the medical center most of the day with my granddaughter Mya and the family as tests took place to determine her problem. She had pain in her leg, which made her limp, and a bad cough with breathing that had become laborious. We hoped for the best, while fearing the worst. Our faith in God was unshakeable at the time. We prayed. We trusted God. All would be well. That faith was soon to be battered by a storm of sickness and sorrow. Would faith endure?

We believed that God is great, and God is good. It is a simple expression in a childhood prayer, and yet a concept so profound that it fills volumes of theology. We taught our children to embrace it, And yet, at times, we would wonder if that reality would slip from our grasp. That was a doubt we would try to lock up in a basement closet, not even daring to whisper it—much like the "c" word. However, even as we would speak of "cancer" of necessity, confronting the grim specter of that notion would haunt us and prove inescapable. It would awaken me in the night, a hideous apparition, that would sneer, "Is God really great and good?"

I think of John the Baptist. He stood on the banks of the Jordan River and thundered a call to repentance. He courageously called out both the ecclesiastical and governmental leaders, naming the Pharisees a brood of vipers and King Herod an adulterer. For this, he was placed on death row, and in the dismal dungeon, the man Jesus described as the greatest man ever born had his faith crisis (Matthew 11:11). The one who proclaimed Jesus as the Lamb of God, would ask, "Are you the Coming One, or do we look for another?" (Matthew 11:3) I once heard the late Vance Havner in a sermon say these words I have never forgotten, "It's one thing to stand on the banks of Jordan and give it, and another to sit in a jail and take it." Likewise, for me to quote the twenty-third Psalm at a funeral seemed helpful, but to share it in preparing for my seven-year old granddaughter's journey into the Valley of Shadow would at times ring hollow.

David decreed,
> *Yea, though I walk through the valley of the shadow of death,*
> *I will fear no evil;*
> *For You are with me;*
> *Your rod and Your staff, they comfort me.* (Psalms 23:4)

INTO THE VALLEY OF SHADOW—*The Journey Begins*

There it is. When a shepherd boy, armed only with a slingshot confronted the ten-foot tall Goliath, he literally walked into the Valley of the Shadow of Death—without fear—for he knew Yahweh, His Shepherd, was with him, able and willing to vanquish his foe. Down went the giant!

What about our giant? Cancer—it loomed over us, larger than the gargantuan Philistine warrior, mocking us as it threatened a sweet little girl who was much smaller than David was. We believed our Good Shepherd would bring down the giant. We knew He was able. Was He willing? Why not? Surely, our prayers would avail as a smooth stone hurled into a giant's forehead—and those malignant cells would crumble to the ground. How God would be glorified! His people, like the armies of ancient Israel would shout with praise that would echo through the valley! They would be emboldened to gain their own victories in seeing the miracle God had wrought with His hand. That was what I thought. Such was our faith as we began the journey into the Valley of Shadow.

Mya's mother, Kelly, wrote these words at the outset,

> Mya is a beautiful and active child. If there is something to swing on, climb, or enough room to turn a cartwheel, you can find her doing it! And do not let her cuteness fool you...she can outrun the boys and keep up with the best of them! You can only imagine our shock and devastation as we spent the last few weeks in and out of doctors' offices and hospitals to finally find out she has stage 3 lymphoma. It has been a whirlwind and only by God's

strength have we been making it through each day. Please join us in prayer.

The Lord strong and mighty,
The Lord mighty in battle. (Psalms 24:8)

Specifically, Mya had Burkitt lymphoma—a rare cancer and a fast growing type—at times a tumor doubling in size in eighteen hours. Her cancer was widespread—a large tumor in her leg, lungs invaded—with one almost full of tumor—and some other places in the abdomen and arm. That was the bad news. The good news was that this cancer was very responsive to chemotherapy—with a cure rate of around ninety percent. That was encouraging. It was the thought of pumping all those toxic chemicals into that frail frame that was concerning. Then there was the math—ninety percent still left ten percent who did not make it—but we tried to dismiss that thought, choosing rather to believe God would heal our baby.

The journey into the Valley of Shadow had begun, and for the better part of a year, we would travel that hard path—and in many ways, our family is still on the road.

Chapter 2

Being Thankful

The Apostle Paul wrote, *"in everything give thanks; for this is the will of God in Christ Jesus for you."* (1 Thessalonians 5:18)

I sat in the hospital room with my little granddaughter, Mya, as she faced a serious battle with illness. I felt anything but thankful. Angry, frustrated, heartbroken, yes, but feeling thankful? Not really.

Therefore, I wondered, "What's up God? How do you expect me to not only endure this trial, but even feel thankful for it?"

That is not what God demands. The command is to be thankful—to choose to express thanks—however we feel. In every situation, it is an opportunity to give thanks. We have a sovereign God—a Father who is perfectly loving, infinitely wise, and all-powerful. Paul said the will of God is *"good and acceptable and perfect"* (Rom. 12:2). I embrace that by faith, not feeling. I don't have to understand. Spurgeon put it this way, in a sermon called, "A Happy Christian"

> The worldling blesses God while he gives him plenty, but the Christian blesses him when he smites

> him: he believes him to be too wise to err and too good to be unkind; he trusts him where he cannot trace him, looks up to him in the darkest hour, and believes that all is well.[1]

The test of an umbrella's quality is not when it is sitting in a corner on a sunny day, but when it is carried into a raging storm. Likewise, fair-weather faith is unproven if untested. Faith is demonstrable only when it is demanded. It was faith that enabled Job to sit in the rubble and ruin of his life and declare, *"The LORD gave, and the LORD has taken away; Blessed be the name of the LORD"* (Job 1:21b).

Here is the reality: God has been good to me—far better than I could deserve. If I got what was coming to me, I would be in hell. We ask, "Why me?" Well, why not me? There have been blessings on top of blessings that I have known in my life, and I daresay that if you will stop and think, you will give thanks too. Some of those blessings may be in disguise. Weigh the message from the song "Blessings" by Laura Story:

> We pray for blessings
> We pray for peace
> Comfort for family, protection while we sleep
> We pray for healing, for prosperity
> We pray for Your mighty hand to ease our suffering
> All the while, You hear each spoken need
> Yet love is way too much to give us lesser things

---

[1] Charles Spurgeon, Metropolitan Tabernacle Pulpit, Vol.13 (Pasadena, TX: Pilgrim Publications, 1989), p.103.

Being Thankful

'Cause what if your blessings come through raindrops
What if Your healing comes through tears
What if the thousand sleepless nights are what it takes to know You're near
What if trials of this life are Your mercies in disguise

We pray for wisdom
Your voice to hear
We cry in anger when we cannot feel You near
We doubt your goodness, we doubt your love
As if every promise from Your Word is not enough
And all the while, You hear each desperate plea
And long that we'd have faith to believe

When friends betray us
When darkness seems to win
We know the pain reminds this heart
That this is not, this is not our home

What if my greatest disappointments
Or the aching of this life
Is the revealing of a greater thirst this world can't satisfy
What if trials of this life
The rain, the storms, the hardest nights
Are your mercies in disguise?[2]

---

[2] Story, Laura. *Blessings*. (New Spring, A Division of Brentwood-Benson Music, 2011)

Chapter 3

Purpose in our Pain

⇢⇢⇢ ❊ ⇠⇠⇠

The chemo treatments were beginning in earnest for Mya, and her mother Kelly wrote,

> The chemo is starting to catch up to Mya. She has felt bad for the last two days. She is keeping a headache and feels nauseous a lot. They are giving her medicine for both and it helps some but if she even sits up, she feels miserable. All the medicines are messing with her emotions too. She had chemo this morning and she gets more at ten tonight, then she has a day off tomorrow. Her last treatment for this go around is the spinal chemo scheduled for Tuesday. If all goes well after that, the doctor expects us to be able to go home for a little while. We are so ready, and she is counting down the days! She says she is ready to play with Tucker (our dog) and sleep in her bed again! It will be so nice to have our family back

together at home again. It has been way too long!
Thank you for the continued prayers.

Those prayers would be needed, for the pain continued, as Kelly would share in her next post:

> Mya is having a lot of jaw and mouth pain. The doctor said her mouth is starting to break down as a side effect of the chemo and will get worse over the next few days. She is having trouble eating and drinking because it hurts to swallow. He said if she cannot keep herself hydrated, then she would not be able to go home. Please pray for her pain to go away and for her to be able to stay hydrated and get to go home. She will be so upset if we have to stay! It is so hard for me to see her hurting and not be able to fix it.

Then Kelly shared the words of a song by the artist Plumb,

> How many times have you heard me cry out, "God please take this?"
> How many times have you given me strength to just keep breathing?
> Oh I need you
> God I need you now![3]

---

[3] Christina Wells, Luke Sheets, and Tiffany Lee. *Need You Now* (Do Right Music, LLC, Mike Curb Music, 2012)

Seeing Mya in pain would always drive us to the perplexing, vexing question of "Why?" Is there a purpose in our pain?

The testimony of the Apostle Paul was, *"Therefore I take pleasure in infirmities, in reproaches, in needs, in persecutions, in distresses, for Christ's sake. For when I am weak, then I am strong."* (2 Corinthians 12:10)

If you find pleasure in pain, then you have a psychological problem! So, how are we to understand what Paul says here? His pleasure is not in the pain itself, but in the purpose for which God permits it and the result that purpose accomplished.

There is something worse than pain—no pain! Pain is designed as a warning system. It alerts us to a problem needing our attention. For example, suppose we never had pain—then we could stand against a hot stove and never realize it was searing our flesh, or we could have an appendix about to rupture and spread deadly infection throughout our body, without being aware of it. Of course, we look forward to a land where there is no pain—a place called heaven! We are not there yet, and so long as we live in this fallen world there will be pain, but for the child of God the purpose our Sovereign Lord accomplishes is worth every hurt. That there are temporal benefits, and eternal blessings, can even bring us to rejoice and glory in our infirmities. That is what Paul is describing in 2 Corinthians 12:1-10.

> *1 It is doubtless not profitable for me to boast. I will come to visions and revelations of the Lord: 2 I know a man in Christ who fourteen years ago—whether in the body I do not know, or whether out of the body I do not know, God knows—such a one*

was caught up to the third heaven. 3 And I know such a man—whether in the body or out of the body I do not know, God knows— 4 how he was caught up into Paradise and heard inexpressible words, which it is not lawful for a man to utter. 5 Of such a one I will boast; yet of myself I will not boast, except in my infirmities. 6 For though I might desire to boast, I will not be a fool; for I will speak the truth. But I refrain, lest anyone should think of me above what he sees me to be or hears from me.

7 And lest I should be exalted above measure by the abundance of the revelations, a thorn in the flesh was given to me, a messenger of Satan to buffet me, lest I be exalted above measure. 8 Concerning this thing I pleaded with the Lord three times that it might depart from me. 9 And He said to me, "My grace is sufficient for you, for My strength is made perfect in weakness." Therefore most gladly I will rather boast in my infirmities, that the power of Christ may rest upon me. 10 Therefore I take pleasure in infirmities, in reproaches, in needs, in persecutions, in distresses, for Christ's sake. For when I am weak, then I am strong.

Paul uses the third person in this testimony and identifies himself as *"a man in Christ"* (v.2). Everything is grounded in this relationship. Being in Christ is transformative. It is an experience all of grace—for we cannot achieve nor deserve such an exalted position. Being in Christ means that all Jesus is has become available to us and God does not see us as we are, but as He views His Son. We may not have had the same experiences as Paul, or the same position as an Apostle, but every believer has the same spiritual standing of being *"in Christ."* It also means that everything that reaches us must first pass through Christ and will help shape us into His image.

Fourteen years previously, Paul had a dramatic experience where he was caught up into the presence of God (v.2-3). He calls it, *"the third heaven"* — not the first heaven, which is the atmosphere where clouds form and birds fly; not the second heaven, which is what we call outer space where the sun and stars shine; but, the third heaven, where God dwells. Whether he was physically or spiritually present not even Paul comprehends. Unlike those who have made a mint in our day describing their heavenly trips, Paul heard things about which he was forbidden to write. The Apostle wanted to glorify God, not himself (v.5-6).

Lest Paul be puffed up with pride, God put a governor on his throttle: *"a thorn in the flesh was given to me, a messenger of Satan to buffet me"* (v.7). The pain was given by a Sovereign God to accomplish His purposes, though Satan provided the delivery service! In this fallen world, God takes even evil and works it together for our good (Romans 8:28).

Paul did what any of us would do — instinctively pray for relief. In fact, this man of faith requests God to remove it three times (v.8). That should say something to the health and wealth preachers of today! God had something better than healing; He gave grace (v.9)! This transformed Paul's perspective on his pain (v.10). When the pain is intense and the prayer for healing denied, learn that it is only because God has a higher purpose.

Writing about these things in theory and experiencing them personally test the sincerity of your faith. It is relatively easy to tell someone else how they should respond to pain, but when it involves you or someone you deeply love, it is another matter altogether.

Throughout this ordeal, my daughter Kelly would continue to lean on the Lord when the pressures at times would threaten to break her. The support and prayers of so many were a constant means of grace for the family. In addition, the grace that God promised was always sufficient.

Chapter 4

God Leads us Along

When God's children walk into the Valley of Shadow, they may be certain that the Good Shepherd has led them there. He does not merely point the way—He walks into the darkness with us. As David testifies of his fearlessness in being harmed in that dark place, his faith is buttressed by other experiences where the Lord had brought him through. Here is one:

> *Have You not kept my feet from falling,*
> *That I may walk before God*
> *In the light of the living?* (Psalms 56:13b)

This verse reminds me of the old song, by George A. Young, "God Leads Us Along."[4] It is a message thoroughly attested by Scripture and affirmed by our experience. The way He leads us, however, may leave us wondering where we are going. The road of life is filled with many twists and turns; we can see but a portion of

---

[4] https://library.timelesstruths.org/music/God_Leads_Us_Along/

the road before us, so we must trust God who knows the destination where He intends to bring us. That is what David discovered on his journey of faith. It is the testimony of Psalm 56.

Our path does not take us through a playground, but a battleground (Psalms 56:1-4)! So long as we are in this world, we will find ourselves in a fight. Our environment is hostile to faith. David—a man of war—would say, "Amen!" The introduction to the Psalm tells us it was written "When the Philistines Captured Him in Gath." Gath was the hometown of the giant Goliath whom David had slain. David was running for his life from King Saul. In a moment of panic, he fled into Philistine territory, and ended up in a place where the people would delight to kill him—out of the frying pan and into the fire! Yet, even so, God had a purpose for David's life. We may wish for, as George Young put it in his aforementioned hymn, "shady green pastures, so rich and so sweet…Where the water's cool flow bathes the weary one's feet…Sometimes on the mount where the sun shines so bright…"[5] and yet find ourselves, "sometimes in the valley in darkest of night that God leads His dear children along."[6]

We may survive the frontal assault and succumb to the surprise attack (Psalms 56:5-7). There were those who would not dare to attack David to his face but would stab him in the back—distorting his words, organizing opposition from the malcontents, and setting snares to trap him. This broke his heart and drove him to the One he could trust, as David cast himself on the promises of God (Psalms 56:8-11). The hymn writer, George Young, again, put it this way:

---

[5] Ibid.

[6] Ibid.

> Though sorrows befall us and evils oppose,
> God leads His dear children along;
> Through grace we can conquer, defeat all our foes,
> God leads His dear children along.
>
> Some through the waters, some through the flood,
> Some through the fire, but all through the blood;
> Some through great sorrow, but God gives a song,
> In the night season and all the day long.[7]

God knows every step we take through dark seasons. He sees every tear we shed as we walk through deep sorrows. According to David, God stores the tears in His bottle and records them in His book! He is mindful of our tears and trials. He does not exempt us from traveling the trail of tears, but He promises grace that is sufficient for the journey now and that our destiny will end in glory.

David expressed confidence that the Lord would establish His feet in the right path and on solid ground (Psalms 56:12-13). He always had; He always would. Young says in his hymn,

> "Away from the mire, and away from the clay,
> God leads His dear children along;
> Away up in glory, eternity's day,
> God leads His dear children along."[8]

The trip may bring many changing conditions in the terrain—sudden storms can break upon us—but one condition never

---

[7] Ibid.

[8] Ibid.

alters—we get there, "all through the blood."[9] The One who died for us will never desert us. He will deliver us!

The next part of Mya's journey would take her out of the hospital and back to the top of the hill on Rory Phillips View—into her house and into her bed for the first time in weeks. A "welcome home" group lined the driveway. We could only wave and yell for her through the window, as her immune system was already compromised, and close contact could not be risked. About that day, Kelly wrote in her journal,

> Mya has had a rough day, but we were able to get home! Hoping that will be good medicine for her! She is not feeling well but Tucker (the dog) got her to smile. Please keep praying. It is going to be a long hard road. So thankful to be home again! And thanks to those who welcomed us up the driveway! We love you!

Yes, it was going to be a long, hard road—this road into the Valley of Shadow. It seemed we had gone far, but there was a long way yet to go. Still, we found consolation that God was leading His dear children along.

---

[9] Ibid.

Chapter 5

Here's Hope!

Your world can be turned upside down in a heartbeat. That is what happened when our little granddaughter, Mya—only six years old at the time—seeming a picture of health and bundle of energy, was diagnosed with cancer. As she fought this deadly enemy, what we desperately sought was hope—and the doctors told us this could be successfully treated. While she seemed to have responded well to the treatments, we knew the immediate future still contained uncertainties. Her mother described one such day:

> We had a follow up appointment this morning and Mya's ANC count, which is her body's ability to fight infection, has almost bottomed out. Some of her other counts are low as well, all which are normal effects of chemo, but still hard. Since her ANC is so low, she is at high risk for infection, so for now we are keeping her in a bubble. She is also having a hard time with nausea and vomiting,

as well as headaches and backaches. They have switched her nausea medication and we are hoping it works! Obviously, all these things are keeping her little body physically exhausted. She has another appointment scheduled for Tuesday morning and they will check her levels again. She will also have more scans next week. If her levels are up enough then they will plan to start her next treatments on Friday, which is our goal. There is a certain window of time that shows better results of chemo, so we really need her counts to be up and able to start therapy Friday. So, the specifics you can pray for are control of nausea and pain, no infections/fevers, rise of blood counts, ability to start therapy next Friday, and we also would love to see more progress on her scans! We are daily, hourly, and most of the time by the minute, trying to cast our cares on HIM! Please remember us.

Hope was being challenged. We knew Mya's future—and ours—was in a hope that does not depend on earth's circumstances, but God's eternal assurances. Ultimately, our hope rests in the Great Physician, Jesus Christ. Do you have such a hope? You can. Titus 2:11-14 tells us how:

> *"For the grace of God that brings salvation has appeared to all men, teaching us that, denying ungodliness and worldly lusts, we should live soberly, righteously, and godly in the present age, looking*

> *for the blessed hope and glorious appearing of our great God and Savior Jesus Christ, who gave Himself for us, that He might redeem us from every lawless deed and purify for Himself His own special people, zealous for good works."*

We see salvation is in three tenses—all bringing hope.

The first tense deals with our past: WE HAVE BEEN PURCHASED (v.11, 14a). I have been saved from the penalty of sin. That is justification. It is the work whereby we are placed in right standing with God by faith in Christ. There are three great Gospel words featured here: *"grace"* and *"salvation"* in verse eleven and *"redeem"* in verse fourteen. The word redemption means to be set free by payment of a price. When Paul wrote these words, men and women were sold in the marketplace like commodities. Spiritually, we were in the slave market, held fast in the shackles of sin. Christ paid the price to free us—and the price He paid was His own blood! He *"gave Himself for us"* and the great exchange took place—Christ took my sins and gave me His righteousness. We were so thankful that included Mya, who, with simple child-like faith—as God requires—had received the gift of eternal life!

The second tense deals with our present: WE ARE BEING PURIFIED (v.12, 14). I am being saved from the power of sin. That is sanctification. It is an on-going process. *"Ungodliness"* is all that is contrary to the nature of God. *"Worldly lusts"* are the perverse passions of our nature that are informed by the putrid philosophies of our culture. These must be denied. Nevertheless, the Christian life is not just about what we avoid, but what we apply: *"We should live soberly"* in our inward disposition, *"righteously"* in our outward demonstration, and *"godly"* in our upward devotion. We must be different to make a difference *"in the present age"* as we are in the world but not of it. A boat is of no use unless it is in the water, but get water in the boat and you are sunk! Paul says that Christ has purified us *"for Himself."* We belong to Him— *"His own special people,"* who are to be *"zealous for good works."* At times, God uses difficulties to be His Heavenly sandpaper to polish us. While we would never have chosen Mya's cancer as the means of His sanctifying us, it has become evident that we were profoundly impacted spiritually by this experience.

The third tense deals with our prospects: WE WILL BE PREPARED (v.13). I will be saved from the presence of sin. That is glorification. I am *"looking for the blessed hope...."* Some golden daybreak Jesus will come! The Savior whom we have heard of, we will we see with our eyes! John wrote, *"everyone who has this hope in him purifies himself, just as He is pure"* (1 John 3:3). The hope in verse thirteen connects with holiness in verses twelve and fourteen. The most important aspect of prophecy is not to give us information about the future, but to bring transformation anticipating it. It is a call to readiness (see 2 Peter 3:10-14). I have always believed in Heaven and preached about the return of Christ, but I will admit that Heaven is more appealing now than before we walked into the Valley of Shadow, and my pleas more urgent and fervent for Jesus to come back for us, than they were before.

Into The Valley of Shadow

Is your hope secure? Does it rest upon Jesus Christ? Remember,

> Only one life;
> 'Twill soon be past;
> Only what's done for Christ, will last. (C.T. Studd)[10]

---

[10] http://cavaliersonly.com/poetry_by_christian_poets_of_the_past/only_one_life_twill_soon_be_past_-_poem_by_ct_studd

Chapter 6

An Attitude of Gratitude

Leading up to Thanksgiving Day, 2015, there were many tough times for our little trooper. Still, we decided an attitude of gratitude was in order. There was much for which we could give God thanks.

Mya set the standard. When many of us would have succumbed to self-pity, she chose to praise God in song. No wonder Jesus used the faith of a child as the standard for His people to seek.

Mya's mom reported these events:

> Mya is feeling good so far this morning. We woke up to bad news that her levels have dropped. We knew it was possible for them to fluctuate but with her burst of energy last night, we were not expecting it. Prayers please that they rise even higher than the minimum one thousand we need to start treatment. We are sitting at one hundred right now—but nothing is impossible for our God.

Into The Valley of Shadow

My sweet girl sings along to this song with me every time we hear it.

> When fear feels bigger than my faith
> And struggles steal my breath away
> When my back's pressed up against the wall
> With the weight of my worries
> Stacked up tall
> You're strong enough to hold it all
>
> I will cast my cares on You
> You're the anchor of my hope
> The only One who's in control
> I will cast my cares on You
> I'll trade the troubles of this world
> For Your peace inside my soul
>
> This was not what I would have chosen
> But You see the future no one knows yet
> And You're still good when
> I can't see the working of Your hands,
> You're holding it all
>
> I'm finding there's freedom
> When I lay it all on Your shoulders
> Cast my cares, I will cast my cares
> I will cast my cares on You
> Cast my cares, I will cast my cares
> I will cast my cares on You[11]

---

[11] Blake Neesmith, Casey Brown, and Sam Tinnesz. *Cast My Cares* (Capitol CMG, 2015)

One of the things we were thankful for was the little friend, Colby, she met in the children's cancer wing. They became big buddies. It is also a joy to report that despite his ups and downs in treatment, that at the time of this writing, Colby is cancer free. He was a ray of sunshine in Mya's life.

Here is how one day unfolded:

> Mya has had some good days and has been full of energy. She has been making laps around this floor and building obstacle courses in the playroom. She and her friend next door, Colby, got remote control cars and have been racing them up and down the halls (those poor nurses! haha!). That has all been fun to watch, and we have laughed a lot! We have been concerned because once her counts dropped, they have just been holding steady. The doctor told us we are starting treatment Monday no matter what her counts are. That means a harder recovery on her next time. But this morning her counts jumped from two hundred to eight hundred. I have tears of joy! Praising Jesus! We are hopeful that tomorrow we will see another increase...our goal of one thousand is in sight! Keep the prayers coming please!

Kelly later wrote:

> Mya started one of her medicines on Monday and the rest is set to start today. These are the hard

hitters. She will have treatment almost all day today, tomorrow, Friday, and Saturday, a break Sunday, and a little more on Monday. We would like to be home for Thanksgiving and as of right now that looks like it might happen! Her levels are up to twelve hundred this morning so that is great! Her PET scan Monday showed that all the tumors are still continuing to respond to the medicines. She is a tough little gal and she has been fighting this hard! She has been feeling really good and going non-stop every day. Of course, today that is all going to change, but at least she got a lot of good exercise and playtime over the last week. We are thankful for that! Thank you to all of you for continuing to pray and, as always, please keep remembering us in your prayers. These medicines are scary and have some terrible possible side effects, but they are helping her body at the same time. Please pray they only help and do not hurt in any way! We love all of you.

There is no place like home! Our Kelly described such a happy day.

We are home and it feels great! Mya is doing so well. This homecoming so far is much better than the last! Hopefully she can enjoy being home this time because she feels much better. She is already playing and laughing—and turning cart wheels in the living room! We have been ready for this day! Thank God for his blessings on our family.

> We are so humbled by the love shown to our family yesterday at the benefit. From the very beginning, everyone has done so much more than we could ask for. A simple thank you does not even feel adequate for all that has been done for our family. We would never choose to walk this road, but to see our family, friends, and community come together for us has been an amazing experience. The Lord has blessed in many ways and we are so thankful. We love you all so much.

As Kelly alluded to, our community and church were steadfast in supporting us. Tens of thousands of dollars were raised to help with the exquisitely expensive cost of cancer treatment. The extravagant offering of prayers exceeded that. Heaven was bombarded with tearful pleading for the healing of our Mya. There is no way to describe the love we felt and how grateful we were for it. God used people as His hands to hold us up in our ordeal.

Another blessing came in our son-in-law, Logan. He was such a strong father through all of this. His employer was also most understanding about his need to be gone from work—though he was able to do some through his computer and by phone, even from Mya's hospital room. Logan had a "whatever it takes" mentality.

He comes from good stock. His father and mother, Royce and Gwenda Phillips, are faithful Christians and active members of the church I serve. They have known the heartache of a child's death. Their son, Rory, was burning brush, when gas fumes ignited, burning him severely. He would not recover, as infection would eventually take his young life. Through it all, this godly couple found a way to thank God through their tears. A grandson, Devan, was stillborn. He was the son of Logan's brother Tyson and his wife Kelly. His little frame is marked by a tombstone in Pole Creek's cemetery—near where Mya's purple casket would later be enclosed in the sod. The Phillips family has suffered much, but a faith that cannot be tested, cannot be trusted. Their anchor holds.

No wonder then that Logan has been such a good husband and father. Kelly spoke of her gratitude to him:

> We had to go back in to the hospital Monday night because Mya was running a fever. Fevers are very common between cycles, but it always means a return trip to the hospital. She is doing well today. This is the first day her stomach has felt better so we are happy about that! She will have blood work each morning and as usual, when her counts are up to one thousand, they will start her next round. I had Mya's sister, Cora, at the doctor yesterday morning, then brother, Rylan, popped up with a fever in the afternoon, and I also have a cold. So, Logan is being "Mr. Mom" at the hospital while I wait on everyone here to get better. He is doing a great job as always! It is nice to have a husband who is such a good father! I married a good one. We are thankful to have been home for a week and to have had Thanksgiving at our house. Please continue praying for us all!

It seemed that time spent at home was only occasional and far too brief. In and out of the hospital, but mostly in. Kelly continued to chronicle those days.

> We are at the clinic waiting on labs and she is getting fluids. If everything is up, then we will be heading to the hospital in about an hour to start her next cycle. I know you are always praying but this treatment makes me even more anxious, so I am going to ask you to pray more than you ever have. Based on her treatment regimen they feel that her cancer should be totally gone after this cycle is complete. They will give it a little time to work and then do more scans to check, and at that time they expect to find nothing. Then she will have one more treatment to make sure nothing small was missed. If following those scans her cancer is still there, then we will discuss further treatment options. There is so much riding on this next cycle and while I hope and pray that it is fully eliminated from her body, I am trying not to be overwhelmed by all the "what ifs" if it's not. Pray, pray, pray that those medicines work as they should, and even more so, that our mighty Healer will restore our little girl to complete health and perfection. She is such a brave little girl and has handled this better than I would have, but she is over it and asking when she is going to be able to stay home forever! And that is just what we want! We know God can make that happen.

What can you do? We thanked God for what He had done and trusted His promises for what He would do.

Chapter 7

Our Keeper

"The LORD is your keeper...." (Psalm 121:5).

God's children are His special treasure. He guards His gems. Peter says we are *"kept by the power of God..."* (1 Peter 1:5). Recently, I saw a quote from Pastor John MacArthur that underscored this, "If you could lose your salvation, you would."[12] God is our Keeper and that is good news! It is also the theme of Psalm 121. Texts like this helped sustain us throughout our journey with Mya into the Valley of Shadow. Perhaps it will be the very source of encouragement you need when you read this today.

The Psalmist points to THE SOURCE OF HELP. Look to Him.

> *"I will lift up my eyes to the hills—From whence comes my help? My help comes from the LORD, Who made heaven and earth"* (v.1-2).

---

[12] https://twitter.com/tgc/status/574038559662829570

Into The Valley of Shadow

It was troubling to look around the hospital room and see all the monitors, tubes, and wires. It was tough to look at the bony arms and baldhead of a sweet little girl. It was terrible to look at the worried expressions on her parents' faces as they were fighting for the life of their baby. They were doing all they could. The doctors could do a lot, but ultimately, we knew that only God could heal. We were helpless to save Mya's life.

When we look around us, we see nothing but problems. When we look within us, we see nothing but inadequacy—or foolishly arrogant self-sufficiency. When we look above us, we find a God mighty to save! As the author would climb the hills to Jerusalem, at last on Mount Zion, he would reach the Temple where dwelt the glory of God. Surely, the One who called into existence the universe by the sheer power of His spoken word can help us—no matter the seeming enormity of our need! That is where we looked for help, and where we continue to fix our gaze for the challenges that remain.

We can know THE STABILITY OF HEAVEN. Stand on Him.

"He will not allow your foot to be moved" (v.3a).

None of us had traveled this path before. We were filled with uncertainty. At times, it felt like we could not stand. The ground was shifting constantly beneath our feet—or so it seemed.

In this world, there are many slippery paths. There are stones aplenty over which to stumble. A fall can be disastrous. Yet, our steps can be steadfast, for God steadies us. He is the Rock—our firm foundation. Just when we felt unsteady, the Lord would show up and through the encouragement of His promises in His precious Word, we could take the next step of faith.

We are comforted by THE SLEEPLESSNESS OF YAHWEH. Rest in Him.

> *"He who keeps you will not slumber. Behold, He who keeps Israel Shall neither slumber nor sleep."* (v.3b-4)

The struggle for sleep was real. You could get so much on your mind as you wondered, "What if...?" Then this truth would act as a sedative for the troubled soul. Why should I stay awake at night—tossing and turning with a mind filled with anxiety? God stays awake, watching over me, so there is no point in both of us being up!

I think of a loving parent, rising in the darkness to look into an infant's cradle, making sure the baby is all right. That is what our Heavenly Father does for us. "Now, I lay me down to sleep; I pray the Lord, my soul to keep." I am sure that during the night watches in Mya's ordeal there were those times that Logan and Kelly would gaze on her as she slept—that is the love of a parent. Nevertheless, even that love could not always overrule the physical exhaustion and demand for sleep. The truth is that Mya always had someone monitoring her—and I do not mean a nurse, though he or she offered remarkable care. The God who sees the sparrow fall was looking down on little Mya, taking note of every heartbeat, hearing every breath.

We are given THE SHELTER OF GOD. Run to Him.

> *"The LORD is your keeper; The LORD is your shade at your right hand. The sun shall not strike you by day, Nor the moon by night."* (v.5-6).

Into The Valley of Shadow

The sun's light need not scorch us by day. The moon's beams need not keep us awake by night. He is the shelter we can find—twenty-four hours a day, through all the days of our life. Sometimes, those years stretch out to seventy and beyond, while for others they may only last for seven. We do not know how long our lifespan will be, but what we are sure of is that the life of God's children is sheltered in His almighty arms.

The sun and moon are symbolic for one day—and thus, we have all day protection. The right hand is mentioned, for it represents human need. God fills that empty hand with His provision—and He does it every day of our lives.

We trust in THE SECURITY OF SALVATION. Trust in Him.

"The LORD shall preserve you from all evil; He shall preserve your soul. The LORD shall preserve your going out and your coming in From this time forth, and even forevermore." (v.7-8).

No evil can destroy the child of God. The most extreme form of cancer cannot really harm us.

That does not mean we are exempt from pain—our body may become sick and death can come. True harm to the real you is not a threat, however, if you know Christ. Our soul will be preserved. No power on earth or scheme of hell can touch the real man or woman we are—our redeemed soul—that dwells in this house of clay. We could not be sure how Mya's disease would respond to treatments. We could not be assured that God would heal her. What we could be confident in was the promise of God's preservation—one way or another.

Actually, the body also will be ultimately preserved, raised in a glorified state in the resurrection. When I leave home in the morning, God travels with me. When I arrive home in the evening, He has been with me. At last, at the end of life's journey, God will usher me into eternity where I will abide in His presence forevermore!

This is our blessed assurance,

> *"Now may the God of peace Himself sanctify you completely; and may your whole spirit, soul, and body be preserved blameless at the coming of our Lord Jesus Christ."* (1 Thessalonians 5:23)

Chapter 8

Above the Storm Clouds

Then I looked, and behold, a Lamb standing on Mount Zion, and with Him one hundred and forty-four thousand, having His Father's name written on their foreheads. (Revelation 14:1)

I remember flying out of Charlotte's airport in the rain. Black clouds enveloped the plane. Powerful engines strained to lift the massive metal jet into the sky. You could not see anything outside the cabin window—all was dark and ominous. Then the plane burst through the clouds into brilliant sunshine. What had been dark clouds overhead became a bed of cotton balls below—bright blue sky all around. That is what happens when you come to the fourteenth chapter of Revelation. The previous chapter has featured flashes of lightning and peals of thunder—the storm of God's wrath having broken on a Christ-rejecting world. It is a scene dark with demons. Suddenly, we gain a new perspective as we are taken into heavenly sunlight. Never forget that as a child of God—no matter the storms of the present—there is a brighter day coming! During the season of storms that engulfed our family during Mya's illness, this reality served as an important reminder—and it still does today.

Above the clouds, we see the glory of heaven:

> *Then I looked, and behold, a Lamb standing on Mount Zion, and with Him one hundred and forty-four thousand, having His Father's name written on their foreheads.* (v.1).

Here are the 144,000 Jews who have been preserved through the tribulation and are now safe in heaven. Though they are the specific ones named, we would not be amiss to see them prefiguring all the elect of God, secure in glory. They, however, are the supporting cast, for the star of the heavenly scene is the Lamb standing on Mount Zion. The spotlight is on Him. That heaven will be an incomparably beautiful place is evident from the Biblical depictions, but what makes heaven out to be glorious is that the Lamb is there! It is the Lamb slain from the foundation of the world who paves the way for us to join Him. It is the Lamb who takes away the sin of the world that purges the wickedness that would bar us. One day we will bow before those nail-scarred feet and join the heavenly hosts singing, *"Worthy is the Lamb that was slain!"*

God has given a birthmark to His children—the seal of the Holy Spirit—that brands us as belonging to Him and guarantees our safe passage into the City of God. In the previous chapter, we have seen Satan has a "Beast-mark" for those who follow the Antichrist. This is a seal which secures their doom—666. The reality is that all of us identify with one group or the other. If God seals me, my eternal destiny is settled. There were 144,000 sealed on earth and there are not 143,999 seen in heaven—all are there and not one was lost! When the roll is called up yonder, I'll be there!

No wonder heaven will be a place of mirth and music:

And I heard a voice from heaven, like the voice of many waters, and like the voice of loud thunder. And I heard the sound of harpists playing their harps. They sang as it were a new song before the throne, before the four living creatures, and the elders; and no one could learn that song except the hundred and forty-four thousand who were redeemed from the earth. (v.2-3).

A sacred symphony of praise will permeate the atmosphere. Note that there will be the singing of new songs. Some of us do not like new songs. Will we enjoy heaven then? Maybe we had better start singing some down here. This is the song of the redeemed and salvation is something to sing about!

Heaven will be more than a happy place—it will be a holy place:

These are the ones who were not defiled with women, for they are virgins. These are the ones who follow the Lamb wherever He goes. These were redeemed from among men, being firstfruits to God and to the Lamb. And in their mouth was found no deceit, for they are without fault before the throne of God. (v.4-5).

The celibacy of the 144,000 may be a literal, physical reality, but it portrays a true, spiritual condition also. These have been morally pure and fully devoted to Christ. They persevered because God purchased them. Their testimony was true. Cleansed by the blood of the Lamb, we will stand faultless and flawless before God—O glorious day!

The next time you look up into a shroud of dark clouds, just remember that above them the sun is shining—and we will gain God's perspective on these storms in the bright light of eternity!

Chapter 9

When the Rug is Jerked out from Under You

After an initial diagnosis that the treatments had worked, and the cancer was in remission, the rug was jerked out from under us. On February 17, 2016, Kelly wrote this:

> I do not even know what to say. Today was a parent's worst nightmare. The last thing I want to do is go into details, but I am because my baby needs your prayers.
>
> My eyes are full of tears, which makes it hard to type. Mya's cancer is back. She starts chemo Friday and we will discuss options about staying here or being transferred. But it is important her treatment start ASAP so the first cycle for sure will be here. In the end, she will have a bone marrow transplant. I do not even know what to think, but we are

> devastated beyond belief. Please, please pray. Our God is the healer and we know he can take this if He just will. We are starting on a long scary road.

It was a journey that none of us would have chosen—a path to be avoided at all costs. That was how we felt, how we thought—a reaction as normal as jerking your hand away from a hot stove burner. I fully realize that our perspective is not God's—that we can trust Him, even "on a long scary road." Surely, He understands too! He knows we do not know what He knows, and that we cannot see what He sees. *"For He knows our frame; He remembers that we are dust."* (Psalms 103:14)

A week later, and the path was no smoother, nor less scary. My daughter chronicled the hard journey.

> Today has not been good. She was sick all night, so we took her to the clinic today to get fluids and more nausea medicine. If she can get rehydrated and is able to keep liquids down, then hopefully she can come back home. She is pitifully sick. But she still gives us that beautiful smile. How I love her. There is nothing like the pain that comes from watching your child suffer and knowing your hands are tied. I wish so badly that God would take this away from her. It is breaking my heart.

I can only say that I am convinced that God's loving heart breaks alongside ours—that He weeps for us, and with us.

Sometimes, the pace of life was so frantic that one had little time to think, and that was not necessarily a bad thing, as those thoughts could quickly become overwhelming. You just do what you have to do on impulse—moment to moment and one day at a time. Kelly documented such a day on March 9, 2016.

> We are in the middle of a crazy busy week! Mya has had multiple appointments and there are many more in the days ahead. So far, she is doing great. She is spinning on the tire swing and enjoying this beautiful weather at the moment! Her PET scan this morning showed that the last cycle of chemo helped, and her leg responded significantly. They said her stem cell levels are terrific, so they plan to do surgery in the morning to place an additional line and then do her stem cell harvest right after that. Her surgery is scheduled for 8:45 so please pray that everything goes smoothly and that she adjusts well to the additional line. We have been told they are kind of stiff and uncomfortable, but we hope she will do well with it. And then also please pray that they are able to harvest enough cells and that she tolerates that procedure well too! The doctor and staff have all been wonderful thus far and we feel encouraged that she is in good hands. We pray that God will oversee each procedure and each person involved in her care and that He will use them to get her well again!

Here was the next day's report:

> Mya's surgery went well, and they were able to harvest enough stem cells, so we are thankful for that good news! She is sore, but we hope that will be much better in the next couple of days. My little girl is tough!
>
> Overwhelmed seems to be the word I use most these days. Everything is overwhelming. But I am trying to just live one day at a time and not worry about tomorrow. I am really missing my boys and having my whole family together. We are just scratching the surface of how much our lives are about to be changed. I have a three-ring binder full of info on how different things will be for a while. It is a lot, but we are so willing to take on this challenge if it means getting our baby healthy again! I struggle with some bitterness. It is hard to see other kids go on with their "normal" life, doing all the things that Mya also loves to do but cannot right now. I really can't wait for the day she is able to live her life again—the life a child should be enjoying instead of being stuck in a hospital bed, taking so many dangerous medications. But I refuse to believe that there will not be a lot of good that comes from this. God has blessed us in so many ways and I know he will see us through this. He is still good, and he is

still faithful, even if I have to remind myself of that all day long.

You can live without food for many days. You can live without water for a few days. You cannot live without hope. Hope was all we had. Hope was enough. It sustained us, and still does.

Chapter 10

UPS AND DOWNS—
The Elevator of Cancer Treatment

A good day is often followed by a bad one, and a bad one by a worse one. Toxic chemicals pumped into the body take their toll. Yet, they are meant to destroy the bad stuff, and when that happens, then respite, recovery, and, prayerfully, remission result. However, one never knows from one day to the next with cancer treatment. It is an elevator, going up and down. One day the sun shines brightly with promise and before the day is over, a thunderclap can announce dark clouds of difficulty descending. I will allow my daughter to eloquently speak of these peaks and valleys, of sunlight and shadow.

March 24, 2016

It has been such a discouraging day. After spending the afternoon at the doctor and having more X-rays, we have found out Mya's leg is now broken. She really has not complained of much pain at all and has been walking and playing. But it is so severely misshaped and has been getting progressively worse over the last couple of weeks. I knew something was wrong. She is tough as nails.

Since we are currently home, the doctors here are getting in touch with the doctors at Duke to see what is going to be best for her. For now, we are home and she's just not allowed to put any weight on it. Please pray even more for her. She just cannot seem to have anything go in her favor lately! And this mama is just about to break so I could use some prayers as well. Our whole family needs them.

April 16, 2016

Mya is on day three of this seven-day chemo cycle. So far, she is managing well. She has been getting a new medicine this time, as well as some she has had before. Tomorrow she will start another medicine that she has had, but it will be three times stronger. She is on a whole line up of chemos, "rescue" drugs, antibiotics, mouthwashes, you name it. It seems like some form of medicine is constantly being forced on her. Most of the time she does well but occasionally she fights it. She is so tired of all of this.

Spring is one of my favorite times of the year. Warmer, longer days. Beautiful blue skies, birds singing and flowers blooming. Planting the garden. Kids playing outside until dark and then having to drag them in and wash the dirt off their little bare feet. Late evenings at the ball field, family whiffle ball games in the yard—things are so different this spring.

I just posted a picture of Mya playing softball, this time last year. That is the Mya I know. That is where we should be spending our time. She loves sports and she just seems to have a natural ability there. God made her who she is...with all her interests and talents in different areas of life. And of course, I am that proud mom. Sometimes I just have to question why those things have temporarily been taken from her. I really want to fix all of this and send her on her happy way back to being a kid and living life. But I cannot. I cannot describe how hard it is to feel so powerless as a mom. I am thankful for a Heavenly Father who holds her and watches over her. He is not powerless. 2 Corinthians 12:9-10 reads:

But he said to me, "My grace is sufficient for you, for my power is made perfect in weakness." Therefore I will boast all the more gladly about my weaknesses, so that Christ's power may rest on me. That is why, for Christ's sake, I delight in weaknesses, in insults, in hardships, in persecutions, in difficulties. For when I am weak, then I am strong.[13]

I need Christ's power to rest on us. I am not going to sit here and lie to you. I can accept parts of this verse, and sometimes all of it. But most days I do not. I do not delight in the fact that my daughter is very sick. I do not delight in the fact that my family has been uprooted and turned upside down. But I can delight in the fact that I have a God who loves me, even when I question Him—a God who can handle my battles; a God who sees every tear and hears every cry in the night; a God who loves my family and isn't going to leave us; a God who knows the beginning and end and is waiting on the other side of this disgusting fight we are facing; a God who promises to give us a future and a hope. I have THE God of the universe holding my family in His hands. Today I will delight in that. He will make me bold and give me strength in my soul.

April 24, 2016

I am currently doing a Bible study on the life of Moses. That is not necessarily a topic I would have picked if I were skimming through devotionals. But I know now that it is by no coincidence that the Lord brought me to it at this time. I feel like I can

---

[13] Holy Bible, New International Version

relate to the Israelites because my family seems to also be wandering in the wilderness. We have not had the comforts of home or a normal life in a long time. I find myself complaining occasionally and asking God why He has brought us here—similar to the questions they asked. But I am reminded that God was leading them to something better and I am trusting Him to do the same for my family. The verse that stood out to me the most this morning was Exodus 14:14 *"The Lord will fight for you, you need only to be still"*.[14] I have no doubt that I will struggle with this, but every day I will give this to Him. And when I take it back, I will try to do it again. I need Him to fight this battle for us.

Today Mya is having a very difficult time. She started having a lot of pain during the night and is very sick today. The effects of the chemo are really hitting her hard. I hate seeing her like this. Please pray for her.

May 6, 2016

Well, unfortunately Mya's counts dropped back down to 0.1 and have stayed there the last two days. Fluctuations are common, but typically, once hers take a little jump they will keep rising—but not this time. We are trying not to be discouraged and are

---

[14] Ibid.

waiting (impatiently) for them to go up and stay that way! We are still finding ways to be thankful, especially over the fact that she feels good. At least that is in her favor while we wait. Mom left today, which is a bummer too. She has been a big help to us, but more than that, I will just miss her company. Praying this weekend brings happy days and higher counts. Engraftment would be a fantastic Mother's Day present!

Chapter 11

Birthday in a Hospital Bed

Life goes on. Sixty minutes become an hour, twenty-four hours turn into a day, and those days become a month, with twelve of them turning into a year. There would be several holidays during Mya's battle that would find her dealing with pain. Cancer does not call a ceasefire on birthdays. Therefore, Mya's seventh and final birthday would roll around, and she would "celebrate" it from a hospital bed. Kelly penned these words on May 11, 2016.

> Today is my sweet girl's seventh birthday! Like most moms with their babies, I remember the day she was born like it was yesterday...what I was wearing that morning, sitting in the waiting room at the doctor's office, eating a pack of the kid's fruit snacks I found in my purse, sending Logan a text at work to ask him if he was ready to meet his baby girl, meeting him at the hospital, and walking in so excited for this day! Then after a pretty easy labor,

she was here! Our beautiful daughter. She was perfect of course. We were so happy and proud, and we loved her so much. And today we are still so happy and proud, and more in love with her than ever before. Thank you, Jesus, for blessing us with Mya Grace.

Psalm 127:3 *Children are gift from the Lord, babies are a reward.*[15]

Mya Grace was indeed a gift—even more precious for the brevity of her lifespan with us. As a jewel is more valuable when it is rare, so her shining smile was so dear, for so soon gone. We did not know what the next days would bring, but we prayed, hoped, wondered, worried, and pressed on into the dark void of the unknown.

It was May 13, 2016, and Kelly shared this:

> There is some minor improvement today. Her temperature is still running high, but the Tylenol is bringing it a little lower than it did yesterday. Her blood cultures are still positive for MRSA. They are hoping to see the antibiotics really kick in strong by tomorrow. She is having some spine pain, but we are praying that it is from cells beginning to engraft, and not from a bone infection. Bone pain is a side effect of engraftment so it is likely and we are praying that is what it is! Her doctor said her

---
[15] The Holy Bible, New Century Version, (Thomas Nelson, 2005)

chances of going to ICU have dropped and it is highly unlikely now, so we are continuing to pray she does not require that either. She is still getting oxygen to assist her breathing. Her oxygen levels are good, but she was breathing too rapidly because of the pain and it was causing her lactic acid levels to rise. The extra oxygen is helping, and those levels have returned to normal as well. She is not out of the woods yet, but we are thankful that today is better than yesterday. Keep praying this infection can be completely cleared from her system and not require any surgery. And please pray her cells engraft and she feels better quickly. Thank you so much for joining us in this fight!

What a battle it was for this little weary warrior!

May 14, 2016

Today has been tough. Mya is still in a lot of pain, which is also making her sick to her stomach, making her heart race, and still preventing her from taking slow, controlled breaths. Her temperature is still staying around 105. So far, the twenty-four hour culture came back negative, so that was great news, and they will continue to monitor it for five days, as well as run more cultures each day. I despise seeing her feel so bad. I cannot even wrap my arms around her because the pain from being touched is too much. Even to touch her bed causes her to cry because of the movement. I want to hold her so badly, but I have to just sit close and look at her. That is hard. Her room is filled with birthday decorations and pictures of her across the years. I see pictures of her the month before she was diagnosed; standing on the beach looking so healthy and beautiful—never knowing what was invading her little body. I hate cancer so much. I hate this life we are presently living. I will praise Him for the good news about the negative culture and I will continue to lift my family to His throne. I am hopeful tomorrow will be better.

Hebrews 4:16 offers this:

So let us come boldly to the throne of our gracious God. There we will receive his mercy and will find grace to help us when we need it most.[16]

Where could we go, but to the Lord?

May 16, 2016

Mya has some sore places breaking out on her skin due to the infection. She is continuing to run a fever and still in a lot of pain. She had a CT scan this afternoon and we have partial results back, which

---

[16] New Living Translation, Tyndale House Publishers

> show that the MRSA infection has gone to her lungs. We have been told it may be days before she begins to improve. The scans of her neck and head are not back yet. She also has some fluid in her lungs. I wanted to share specifics so that you could help us pray. It is very hard to see her like this. Please pray for healing and for the medications to work effectively and quickly—and destroy every last bit of this infection!

I recall how concerned I was in those days. Being a pastor, I had far too much experience with people dealing with cancer, and ultimately dying from it—or from an infection developed because of the devastating effects of chemotherapy on the body's immune system. It was a justifiable concern.

<u>May 17, 2016</u>

> We are begging you to pray with all urgency. Mya has developed a serious pneumonia from the staph infection. They are going to take cells from her daddy and try to give them to her later this week to help her fight this, because she just can't do it. Logan would literally give her his lungs if he could take this away, so it was no question when they asked if he would be willing to do this. Obviously, there are risks to her and to him, but this has to be done. Hopefully this buys some time until she can

make her own, but we do not have much time to buy because her cancer is such a fast-growing type.

It is so hard. I want to throw myself on this hospital floor and scream. But I have to suck it up and be strong for her, until she goes to sleep. Then the tears do not stop. I am beginning to question God in his plan for this. It just does not make sense. I need prayers to trust Him because I am really struggling right now.

Chapter 12

Better and Brighter Days

Halfway through the month of May, things began to improve. Some encouragement gave rise to even more hope. Rays of sunshine were breaking through the clouds. For the first time in days, I really thought Mya Grace was going to lick this thing—that the miracle so many prayed for was unfolding.

Kelly wrote:

<u>May 18, 2016</u>

> Today we were so thankful to get some good news. Her white blood count was 0.3 last night, 0.2 this morning, and that is not much but it is up from 0.1 which shows her body is beginning to make more white blood cells. She also tested negative for the rhinovirus, which she has been positive for since we got here, so that also shows she is making white blood cells to fight off that infection. She made it

through the night without Tylenol and no fever! That is a huge blessing. She has been running a fever today, but it is staying in the 102 range, which is much lower than the 105.8 it had been! And she has actually wanted me in the bed with her, so I have been blessed to hold my baby girl. To have the doctors come in with a little encouragement was such a good feeling. They were able to harvest Logan's white blood cells this morning, take the granulocytes out, and give those to Mya this afternoon. She finished receiving those about two hours ago and hopefully they are on their way to help fight this terrible infection. She will get two more cycles of those over the next two days. It is mind boggling to think about how they are able to do something like that. We are thankful for the technology and knowledge that fuels the medical field today.

We know so many are standing with us in prayer for Mya. God is carrying us through. I know that God is above and beyond our circumstances. They do not change who He is. He is still a good, good Father. The pain, fear, doubts, questions—they all remain. This earth is not our home.

Please keep praying for us all. She is still very sick, and she has a long way to go, but we are hopeful. Mya is a fighter.

Kelly would then go on to share this song:

"Broken Hallelujah" by Mandisa--

With my love and my sadness
I come before You Lord
My heart's in a thousand pieces
Maybe even more

Yet I trust in this moment
You're with me somehow
And You've always been faithful
So Lord even now

When all that I can sing
Is a broken hallelujah
When my only offering
Is shattered praise
Still a song of adoration
Will rise up from these ruins
I will worship You and give You thanks
Even when my only praise
Is a broken hallelujah

Oh Father, You have given
Much more than I deserve
And I have felt Your hand of blessing
On me at every turn

Into The Valley of Shadow

>How could I doubt Your goodness
>Your wisdom, Your grace
>So Lord hear my heart
>In this painful place
>
>When all that I can sing
>Is a broken hallelujah
>When my only offering
>Is shattered praise
>Still a song of adoration
>Will rise up from these ruins
>I will worship You and give You thanks
>Even when my only praise
>Is a broken hallelujah[17]

The "hallelujahs" continued to be expressed as more encouraging news came day by day.

May 20, 2016

>Mya is having a MUCH better day. Thank you, God! She is still not running a fever, and she was able to come off the oxygen! She has been walking to the bathroom instead of being carried, and she is on the couch instead of the bed! We have been blowing bubbles to work on those lungs and I am hoping to get her to take a couple of slow strolls in the hallway

---

[17] Wood, Tony, Gina C. Boe, Ronnie Freeman Broken Hallelujah - (CMG Song# 48963) Copyright © 2009 New Spring Publishing Inc. (ASCAP) Row J Seat 9 Songs (ASCAP) Lehajoes Music (ASCAP) Write About Jesus Music (ASCAP) (adm. at CapitolCMGPublishing.com) All rights reserved. Used by permission.

with me later this evening. She is getting the last batch of cells as I type and resting peacefully. It is so nice to see that—instead of seeing her struggling even when she was asleep, like she did a couple days ago. Her white blood count is up a lot and we knew Logan's cells would cause that, but they continue to increase each night, so we have reason to believe that a good portion of those are her cells and not his. The labs at midnight Sunday will give us a better picture of what her WBC count is because by then his should be totally out of her system. We are praying she's engrafting! She is going to have another CT scan Wednesday to see how her lungs are responding. I pray the infection will be completely gone! Thank you so much for continuing to pray with us. She needs them! Please praise the Lord with us for the improvements she is making!

Another issue Mya would face was pneumonia—among her many challenges. So, on May 24, 2016, Kelly wrote:

Mya's WBC count was 1.4 today and those are all hers! She should continue to rise now. We are so thankful! She is improving with each day. She has even been able to ride the bike a little in the hallway. As sick as she was just a few days ago, we know this is absolutely an answer to prayer. We have witnessed a miracle. God has blessed her with healing, and we are so glad! She will have another CT scan later this week to see how things are looking but based on how she is feeling we expect to see great improvement! Please pray that there are no lasting side effects. There is some permanent lung damage that can result from this type of pneumonia so they will monitor that as time goes on, but they said not everyone has it, so we pray she does not! They also are trying to decide how long to treat the pneumonia, so pray for God to give them wisdom in that decision too. Thank you so much for praying!

May 25, 2016

Mya is officially engrafted! Today was day 3 of her WBC count being up, so we know now that her cells are going to continue growing. We have been waiting for this day! She had another CT scan today and I think it would be safe to say they were amazed at how much she has improved. They guessed the infection to be about ninety percent gone! Praise the Lord! Keep praying for it to totally clear, for no lasting side effects, and for her stomach to feel better. She is having some trouble with nausea and stomach pain. But she is a different child compared to last week, and we are very thankful for how well she is doing!

May 28, 2016

> Things are going well! Mya was able to "leave" on pass today for two hours, so we went out to the courtyard and she enjoyed being outside for the first time in seven weeks! She is really feeling good and they are planning to discharge her on Tuesday, if things continue to improve. Our leash will be somewhat short but just to be out of the hospital will be so great (we might even get to sneak in a couple days at home)! We cannot wait. Keep praying!

Oh, the things we take for granted! Imagine what it feels like for a soft spring breeze to blow on your face, to hear birds singing in the trees, and to see grass growing green under a warm sun! When those things have been denied you for weeks of beeping monitors, stale hospital smells, tubes and tests, and all the rest—what joy to experience the wonder of simple things. Then, came this celebration on the last day of May.

> Mya was discharged today! We are so thankful to have her here with us. Radiation is next. It will start in a couple of weeks and be daily for 3 weeks. It is not something that is typically used for lymphoma, so the doctors are trying to come up with the best way of using it as part of her treatment. They want to give her cells another form of therapy that it has not seen before. It really makes me nervous! Please be praying that they are able to target exactly the

Into The Valley of Shadow

areas where the cancer was/is and nothing more. It can be very damaging, and I just pray that God protects her body from the possible negative side effects and that it only helps and doesn't hurt in any way—and that her organs, spine and growth plate are protected. Please pray that this is an effective treatment for her. Also, please be praying for her energy levels and appetite to increase. She really tires out quickly, which is expected. But it is also hard for her not to be able to do the things she used to! And she is currently still on TPN, which is the IV nutrition for twelve hours a day. We need her appetite to increase so she can maintain her weight without needing to continue this. Thank you for praying!

On May 31, Mya was celebrating going home to be with us. Little did we know that it would be such a brief stopover on the way to her real home above.

Chapter 13

Descent into Darkness

Remission! What a wonderful word! Nevertheless, we had heard them before. Remission does not mean cured. It means a respite—and with this cancer, the respite would be exceedingly brief. We were about to descend into the darkest days—a month and a half that would in some ways seem eternal and yet all too soon over.

The month began on an upbeat note.

June 5, 2016

> So far, radiation is going well. Tomorrow they will be adding her stomach to the treatment and that can cause some nausea and irritation, but not always. Please pray that it does not and that she is able to continue eating. Her appetite is definitely beginning to increase, and we do not want a set back with that. Having her here with us is such a great feeling!

Into The Valley of Shadow

> We have been able to have somewhat of a normal weekend. She enjoyed getting to watch her older brother Isaiah play ball—and yesterday we made the trip to watch the Enka High School Sugar Jets softball team win the state championship! It was less than an hour from our house and she wanted to go. Outdoor activities are her only option right now because of germs, so she really enjoyed being able to do that! The team really went out of their way to accommodate us and made her feel so special. She said she is going to play for them one day! God is good and He is blessing us with some great family time together. So thankful for that. Keep praying!

Precious memories were being made. They are painful, yet precious. A few more good days and then things would dramatically deteriorate. Perhaps, you have heard it said that the darkest hour is before the dawn—in this case, the brightest days would be before the night.

<u>June 9, 2016</u>

> Prayers are being answered! We are half way through radiation and side effects have been minimal so far. She has had some nausea and heartburn, but it has been manageable. Morning and night are the times she complains the most, but even then, it is temporary. The doctor today said everyone is amazed at how well she is doing. We know it is God.

Descent into Darkness

He made her with such a determined personality. If Mya wants to do something, she will find a way! In these situations, that is a blessing! That, along with his grace, are helping her every day.

<u>June 13, 2016</u>

Only four more days of radiation to go! We are so ready to get it over with. Today, they discontinued TPN for Mya, which is great news! She will be able to stay off of it as long as she maintains her weight, but we would like for you to pray that she gains weight. Forty pounds for a seven-year-old is tiny. They also have stopped one of her antibiotics, which is good news too. Her surgery to have this central line removed is scheduled for next Tuesday. Please pray that goes well. It is pretty routine, but still surgery! Then after that, we should be able to come home for a few weeks. We are so excited for that!

We do not have transplant definite possibilities yet. We found out that there are five donor matches for her, but two have declined and three have not responded yet. They will not give them much longer to reply because we will need to begin the preparations for the transplant soon. So, if they do not hear back, then we will proceed with a cord blood transplant. It is still a great option for her. The potential

> down side is that it can take longer to engraft, which will leave her more susceptible to infection. But we can pray about that too! We are remaining hopeful and trusting God with it. I have prayed from the beginning that whichever transplant she gets, that it will be her best match and what will work the best for her. Please pray with us about all of these things! We are thankful for how far she has come and that she is feeling so well!

Father's Day, June 19, 2016, was celebrated around my fire pit in the backyard. Mya was there, eating s'mores. How I wish I had held her longer! How I wish I had caressed her and kissed her and smelled her soft child's skin. I did not know that this would be her last trip to Papa's, or I would have wrung out of that day every second of meaning.

On June 21, Kelly wrote,

> Headed home after she had her surgery to take her line out so she could spend her summer swimming. She pulled her two front teeth on the ride home. Never would have believed we would be back in the hospital by the weekend.

Moreover, she would never get to swim. My only consolation is that she may be splashing in the crystal river that flows from the throne of God. I like to think so.

June 24, 2016

> Surgery went well and we are home. Overall, she is doing well but she is still losing weight and her leg is really bothering her. She is having some nausea too, which could be a delayed side effect of the radiation she had to her stomach. If you would please pray for those things, we would appreciate it. We really want her to enjoy her time out of treatment and being at home! And we need her to regain as much strength as possible before going into the next transplant. Thank you for praying.

June 27, 2016, and the tide turned to the bad—a tsunami of horror would wash over us.

> This is hard. We have had a big scare this weekend. Mya was admitted to the hospital but is back home now. There are some concerns. She will have appointments this week and a PET scan too. I am scared senseless. Just when I think I can breathe I get the wind knocked out of me again. Please pray for us as we face this week.

Mya began having chest pains and would be taken back to the hospital.

> Pleading for your prayers. Mya is having extreme stomach pain and vomiting. She has been readmitted

> to the hospital and has a PET scan at 9:30 in the morning. There are some concerns with her blood work. Please beg God for an answer other than the one we are fearing the most. We desperately want good news tomorrow. Our hearts are so heavy.

Mya would leave her house—for the last time. She would go to the hospital, never to return. I can walk into the waiting area of the children's wing, close my eyes, and still feel her there. I go back to her house and Mya is everywhere: the trampoline she jumped on, the swing set she swung on, the bed she slept in—in a room full of her dolls and clothes, the table she ate at, and the pictures—her sweet smile beaming from the walls. She is gone, but she is not. Memories remain. The influence of her life warms this cruel world still. She cannot come to us, but we can go to her. Mya would not enter the door of her house on the hill again when she left, but we will enter her house in heaven someday and never leave. Sad partings, happy greetings!

When Mya was readmitted, our worst fears would be realized. At the time, here were my thoughts as I posted them on Facebook on June 29, 2016.

> At times, I want to punch the wall, and at other times feel like I have been punched in the gut. There are moments when I am so full that tears spill over my eyelids and cascade down my cheeks, and minutes later feel utterly empty, dried up, and withered. The news we received yesterday about Mya was brutal. Her cancer is back—the dreaded diagnosis we did

Descent into Darkness

not want to hear. She has fought so hard, suffered so much — a tiny girl with the heart of a lion! Now, she is in the biggest battle of her life. Will you join us in that fight, by praying for her? Thank you in advance. *"Now I beg you, brethren, through the Lord Jesus Christ, and through the love of the Spirit, that you strive together with me in prayers to God for me..."* (Romans 15:30).

More treatments would be prescribed, more toxins injected. Her little body would not take it — there had been too much. The decision was made to stop the treatment. It would kill her. We would pray for a miracle. It was in God's hands — Mya was in God's hands. We tried everything. Someone suggested essential oils, so we got her a diffuser that would fill the air in her hospital room with fragrance.

Her appetite was not much. One day she asked for a steak, and I hustled to Texas Roadhouse and eagerly paid for one. Taking it to her, she ate a few bites. I suppose that was the last food she ate. In fact, I remember telling her that Papa would not eat again until she was able to eat — and so I entered into a time of fasting and prayer. Logan and Kelly called for the elders of the church to come, anoint her with oil and pray for her. Tearfully, we did, and ended our time singing with broken-voices, "Jesus loves me, this I know...". [18]

Her healing was not to be.

---

[18] Warner, Anna Bartlett. *Jesus Loves Me, This I Know* (public domain)

Chapter 14

Final Days

I held out hope until the end. We believed that with God all things are possible.

The doctors were not encouraging. They were not being mean—just honest. Kelly would write these awful words,

> "It won't be long." Those are words that no parent wants to hear. But as I lay here next to my precious child and watch her struggle to take every breath, I am more painfully aware that it is true. I have never despised something as much as this. I have begged God every hour of every day to please heal her. Yet through it all, I am confident of this—when she meets Him, she will be healed. And He reminded me of this "it won't be long". Hearing those words from Jesus is much sweeter than hearing it from a doctor. Because He tells me *"But do not forget this one thing, dear friends: With the Lord a day is like*

a thousand years, and a thousand years are like a day."[19] So, while I will hurt like I never have before and I will miss her like crazy, from her perspective in Heaven, Mama will be there by the end of the day. I love you sweet angel baby. It will not be long. God give my family strength and comfort.

During this time, our family was facing more crises. Our youngest son, Corey, was in drug rehab in Georgia, and my father was fast fading. I went to see him, and he was barely hanging on. Marilyn and I traveled around suppertime to the hospital to visit Mya, and we had no more gotten there until we got the call that Dad was dead.

Somewhere along the way, I picked up a bug, and began to cough. Just worn down, I guess. I knew that I could not go in to see Mya, for what sliver of possibility of recovery remained, would certainly end if she contracted the crud I had. Therefore, I was unable to even visit with her the last few days. I sat in my car in Mission hospital parking lot, waiting as Marilyn went in to see Mya. I desperately wanted to—I wanted to kiss her, knowing she was so low and yet holding out hope in a God of miracles to do one yet. I was not going to be responsible for ending her life, so I waited.

When Marilyn returned, we left for the hot pinewoods of Georgia. Our youngest son was graduating the next day from the drug rehab program. Not everyone knew that in the midst of my father's decline and demise along with Mya's struggle that we were dealing with a child who had been hooked on drugs.

---

[19] 2 Peter 3:8, The New International Version

As we were in some small Georgia town, Marilyn received a text that Mya's time was short. I pulled over into a fast food parking lot and called. I asked that the phone be placed near Mya's ear and Marilyn and I talked to her through our tears. Mya's breathing was so hard—we could hear her little groans—and with each one—it felt like a knife repeatedly stabbed into my chest. We told her so sincerely, so repeatedly, how much we loved her and how we would miss her. As her pastor as well as her Papa, I reassured her that Jesus was there, and He would care for His little lamb. I have stood at the bedside of many dying and sought to comfort them with the hope of heaven, but this was different—it was my baby girl's little girl. I felt so inadequate, so helpless.

Sometimes prayers are sighed when they cannot be said. *"Likewise the Spirit also helps in our weaknesses. For we do not know what we should pray for as we ought, but the Spirit Himself makes intercession for us with groanings which cannot be uttered."* (Romans 8:26). The Spirit of God takes our groans and shapes them into prayers. He pleads for us when we do not know what to pray. The Father receives those groans, translated into intercession for us by the Spirit—always in the will of God and thus received. *"Now He who searches the hearts knows what the mind of the Spirit is, because He makes intercession for the saints according to the will of God."* (Romans 8:27)

Frankly, those sighs that produced our sobs have haunted me for some time. Then, it dawned on me—Mya was praying! The Holy Spirit would translate those sighs into something perhaps like this, "Dear Jesus, I love my family and look forward to seeing them again someday. Right now, I am ready to leave my mother's arms and be received into Yours. The pain here is too much. I want

Final Days

it over. The pleasures that await are so exciting! I asked my father and mother if we could ride dolphins in heaven. Can we? I'm ready to find out!"

Moreover, we wept and cried, "Baby, Papa and Nana love you! We'll see you later." Therefore, we will!

By the time we reached our destination, Mya had reached her final destination. Pulling into the bed and breakfast where we were staying, fighting back tears every moment—such a heaviness pressing on me—I saw beside where I parked, a child's wagon turned on its side. How apropos! Our world seemed wrecked.

Would God's grace be enough?

> "Through many dangers, toils and snares,
> I have already come;
> 'Tis grace hath brought me safe thus far,
> And grace will lead me home."[20]

God's grace has been enough, it will be enough, and at last, that grace will be enough for me to join Mya in heaven.

On one Saturday, I would officiate at my father's funeral. On the next Saturday, I would conduct my granddaughter's. Dad had lived a long life. He had suffered much and become just the shell of what he once was. Heaven was the place he longed for and sung about throughout his many days of music ministry in the church. There were some tears, but also great rejoicing that he was free from the body and mind that no longer worked. But Mya—so young, so full of life, fighting so hard to be well, and so many years, we hoped, in front of her—so much she had yet to experience. Her

---

[20] Newton, John. *Amazing Grace* (public domain)

dad would never walk her down an aisle to wed some boy she would someday come to love. I would never be able to officiate at that wedding, and cry as I always do. However, I would cry and cry and cry, not for what was, but for what would never be.

Chapter 15

Uncle Caleb

Mya's Uncle Caleb posted these words on the morning of her funeral.

Today we celebrate Mya's life.

> The old saying goes, "You don't know what you've got till it's gone." I always knew that I loved Mya, but I never understood the depth of that love until I was faced with losing it. As painful as it is to admit, we take our loved ones for granted. We do not savor the little moments with them near as often as we should. The aforementioned cliché would not exist if that were not true.
>
> But thankfully, we do still have moments and memories despite our foolishness. One of the grandest that I have with her is also one of the most recent.

On the 4th of July, I stood in her hospital room and fought back tears as I prepared to return to Charlotte. As my older brother can also attest, it is not easy living in another city when your family needs you back home. It is even harder when this could potentially be your last time with one of them.

I hugged and said goodbye to those who were there and went over to her bed. I kissed her and explained to her that I was going back to Charlotte as she tapped away on her Kindle. I told her I loved her and stood to leave as a small, raspy voice from below replied, "I love you too."

Those would prove to be the last words Mya ever said to me.

I also remember on one particular drive up the mountain to see her, I saw a rainbow. Brilliant at first but fading more and more as I drove on. It reminded me of God's promise to Noah. It reminded me that He is still there and that He is true to His word. And perhaps I was a fool desperately searching for a sign from above, but it gave me hope that He would heal her.

When I got to Mya's room, the weight of her condition fell heavy on my soul. Like the beautiful rainbow I watched dissipate above me, Mya's health had significantly declined. The colorful, vibrant 7-year-old was quickly fading away.

But although the rainbow may fade, God's promise does not.

> Our Father in Heaven knows what it is like to lose a child. His only Son was mocked, beaten, and slain for the sins of this world. Jesus may have faded on the cross, but God's promise did not. Hallelujah, the grave could not hold Him! And because of Mya's faith in that resurrection, the grave cannot hold her. We will weep because we miss her dearly, but we will not shed a tear for where she is.
>
> Logan and Kelly will hold their baby girl again. Her grandparents will once again laugh and play with her. And I will have all of eternity to pester her just like I do the rest of my nieces and nephews. That is what uncles are for.
>
> But today we celebrate Mya's life. We remember the love and laughter that little girl brought into our lives. We cling to the memories and to God's promises. We vow to live each day with the courage, the resiliency, the child-like faith of Mighty Mya.
>
> Above all else, we give thanks to the One who formed her, redeemed her, and paved a golden path so that we might find her once again.

We love you, Mya.

"Let me be singing when the evening comes."[21]

---

[21] Lyrics.com, STANDS4 LLC, 2019. **"10,000 Reasons (Bless the Lord) Lyrics."** Accessed August 5, 2019. https://www.lyrics.com/lyric/35345919/Matt+Redman.

CHAPTER 16

MIGHTY MYA—
A CELEBRATION OF HER LIFE

We have had women in our church whose husbands have passed away. We call them widows. When men lose their wives, we describe them as widowers. Children whose parents die are called orphans. When a child dies, there is no name for the parents left behind. We have no word to describe that because it is not supposed to happen. It is against the natural order of things.[22] What should happen is that Mya would attend my funeral in a decade or two, not that I would officiate at her funeral. We are trapped in a nightmare from which we cannot awaken.

If you have come here today looking for some explanation for why a sweet little girl would suffer and die, then you will be disappointed—I am fresh out of answers.

---

[22] I am indebted to Levi Lusko for this thought from his heart-moving story of the death of his daughter recorded in, "Through the Eyes of a Lion," (Thomas Nelson), p.37.

Into The Valley of Shadow

Perhaps you recall the movie *Rudy*. Rudy wanted nothing more in life than to play football for Notre Dame. Being undersized, he cast himself upon divine intervention and went into the chapel to pray. When the kind priest asked Rudy how he could help, Rudy expressed his desire to play for Notre Dame. The priest answered, "Son, in thirty-five years of religious study, I've come up with only two hard, incontrovertible facts; there is a God, and, I'm not Him." [23] I want you to know I believe there is a God who has the answers, but I am not Him.

However, even if we had answers, would they be sufficient to take away our pain? If you broke your leg—a compound fracture—for the doctor to explain the density of bones, and how they fracture, a detailed discussion of how to set one, and so forth—would that make your leg hurt any less? So, if God explained all that He knows would our hearts ache any less? I think not.

Instead, God directs us to Himself—to trust Him, to lean on Him and each other in love, to anchor our souls in hope in the midst of this storm. He is with us in the eye of the hurricane of horror.

When our youngest son, Corey, was small, he broke his arm. I accompanied him to the X-Ray room. Of course, I had to wait outside while a heavy wooden door separated me from my boy. They stretched out his broken arm and I heard him scream. He kept calling, "Daddy! Daddy! Help me!" I was there even though he could not see me, and I knew this was necessary although you could never have convinced him. I knew things he did not. I knew this had to be and I wept with him. Therefore, when someone asks, where God is in

---

[23] RUDY
© 1993 TriStar Pictures, Inc.
All Rights Reserved.
Courtesy of TriStar Pictures

all this—I want you to know that even though you might not have seen him and He did not come to the rescue as we begged, He was there and grieved with us.

So, I am not here to defend God. He can handle Himself. I am here to encourage you and pray the Holy Spirit would bring comfort through this message. As Peter said, *"always be ready to give a defense to everyone who asks you a reason for the hope that is in you…"* (1 Peter 3:15). I am here to give a defense for hope.

Mighty Mya—they did not call her that because of her height, but because of her heart.

I want you to know where that strength came from. First, it came from Jesus. She loved Him—sang His praises and called on His name—and now has seen Him face to face. The promise of Philippians 4:13 was a reality in her, *"I can do all things through Christ who strengthens me."* That power flowed to her through the conduit of courage residing in her father and mother. If you have ever been around her Dad, you have seen a man with an unfailing desire to succeed—whether it was the effort he put in on the ball field and gym floor, or his sales efforts. I have told people that Logan could sell ice to an Eskimo. He took that same commitment and courage to help give his daughter every possibility of getting well. Then, I think of my sweet Kelly. Christians should be marked by three supreme virtues—faith, hope, and love. I have been amazed at how these have been seen in my baby daughter. Her faith in God has been tested in the fire, but emerged as pure gold. Her hope has been buffeted by a typhoon of trouble, yet the anchor holds. Her love for the Lord and her Mya are beyond dispute—clearly seen through it all.

God placed that little baby in your womb, Kelly—the precious product of your and Logan's love. Then at Mission Hospital, she

Into The Valley of Shadow

entered this world to be placed in your arms on May 11, 2009. It could have been your death—you lost so much blood. Now, from that same hospital, on the same G Wing, just a floor below, Mya was again in your arms, when Jesus entered the room and took her into His on July 14, 2016. And again, you felt like you would die.

Some races are a sprint while others are a marathon. Mya was a sprinter. Her speed was exceptional. She was a winner. Cancer did not win. It slowed her down, it put up hurdles for her to clear—but she did, and has crossed the finish line in heaven!

On Father's Day, my granddaughter Josie gave me a perfect gift—a Tar Heel cup, stuffed with a big Habanero Slim Jim and a bunch of Cow Tales. I love Cow Tales; it is my candy of choice for two reasons—they are sweet and cheap. I quickly consumed most of them. Nevertheless, only a few days later, Mya's condition declined, and the doctors gave her minimal chance of survival. I decided to fast and pray until she got well one way or another. Mya was soon so sick and unable to eat. I remember kneeling by her hospital bed and whispering in her ear, "Papa is not going to eat again until you get well and can eat." Returning home, I put the one remaining Cow Tale in my desk drawer—and forgot it. Thursday morning, as I was reading, I reached in that drawer for a highlighter and saw that Cow Tale. I always loved to buy them and share them with the grandkids at the baseball field, football stadium, or gym, which we frequented a lot. I took it out, opened the wrapper and remembered Mya—and thought, "This is for you, Mya," and ate it in her honor. Now all that remains is the wrapper—the sweetness inside is gone. Bear in mind, as we do what seems the unbearable today, and take this casket to be encased in the earth, that all it contains is the wrapper Mya used to live in. The sweetness inside is gone—who she really is has left as Paul said in 2 Corinthians 4:16-5:8:

> *Therefore we do not lose heart. Even though our outward man is perishing, yet the inward man is being renewed day by day. For our light affliction, which is but for a moment, is working for us a far more exceeding and eternal weight of glory, while we do not look at the things which are seen, but at the things which are not seen. For the things which are seen are temporary, but the things which are not seen are eternal. For we know that if our earthly house, this tent, is destroyed, we have a building from God, a house not made with hands, eternal in the heavens. For in this we groan, earnestly desiring to be clothed with our habitation which is from heaven, if indeed, having been clothed, we shall not be found naked. For we who are in this tent groan, being burdened, not because we want to be unclothed, but further clothed, that mortality may be swallowed up by life. Now He who has prepared us for this very thing is God, who also has given us the Spirit as a guarantee. So we are always confident, knowing that while we are at home in the body we are absent from the Lord. For we walk by faith, not by sight. We are confident, yes, well pleased rather to be absent from the body and to be present with the Lord.*

Let us embrace our tears and accept permission to grieve. This is a brutal business we are facing, and I cannot think of a worse thing than to stifle the expression of sorrow. That is physically harmful. It is why you hurt and feel like you are choking when you try to hold back the tears. Tears contain toxins that need to be released. Think of it as God's pressure valve that He designed to vent the sorrow that rises up within us. *"Jesus wept,"* (John 11:35), and we may follow His example. Jesus said, *"Blessed are those who mourn, for they shall be comforted"* (Matthew 5:4). If you want the solace of God, then you must be willing to express sorrow to God. It is a humbling acknowledgment of our desperation, but the Bible says, *"[God] gives grace to the humble"* (Proverbs 3:34b). We need that grace! We cannot stand if He does not hold us up! However, *"underneath are the everlasting arms"* (Deuteronomy 33:27a). God takes our tears and treasures them, placing them into His bottle (Psalms 56:8).

> It is a known fact that in Bible lands and other middle eastern countries there was a tradition that when someone died, tears of those present were collected and placed in a bottle. This bottle was considered sacred for it represented all the sorrow of the family and was buried with the deceased. Many of these bottles have been found in ancient tombs. In ancient Rome, mourners filled small glass vials or cups with tears and placed them in burial tombs as symbols of love and respect. Sometimes people were even paid to cry into cups, as they walked along the mourning procession. Those crying the

loudest and producing the most tears received the most compensation. The more anguish and tears produced, the more important and valued the deceased person was perceived to be. In some war stories, women were said to have cried into tear bottles and saved them until their husbands returned. Their collected tears would show the men how much they were loved and missed.[24]

We prayed for a miracle—and God did perform miracles in Mya's life:

- He extended her time.

The healing we receive in this world is never "perfect healing," as I saw some express in prayer for her across the months. I appreciate the sentiment and know they meant restored fully to health and vitality. However, all healing is an extension of time—and at some point, to face sickness and death again. Perhaps this is one reason Jesus wept for Lazarus. He was calling him back to a world of suffering and sorrow—having been four days in paradise and now reentering a world of woe, to have to die again. He was healed—raised from the dead—but it was only an extension of time.

- He used her to inspire and encourage.

I cannot begin to tell you the number of Facebook posts, emails, texts, cards, calls, and personal conversations where thousands

---
[24] http://www.jlfoundation.net/tears-in-a-bottle.html

have told me how Mya has inspired them. Her smiling face was all over the internet—and it was particularly heartening to hear from those who had children who also died or those who were currently dealing with cancer themselves to say that Mya's story was such a blessing to them.

- He refined our faith in the fire.

Peter wrote to suffering saints who were facing persecution for their faith. He said this, *"In this you greatly rejoice, though now for a little while, if need be, you have been grieved by various trials, that the genuineness of your faith, being much more precious than gold that perishes, though it is tested by fire, may be found to praise, honor, and glory at the revelation of Jesus Christ,"* (1 Peter 1:6-7). A faith that cannot be tested is a faith that cannot be trusted.

- He strengthened our hope.

The believer's hope is anchored in eternity. This world is never our home. We are reminded of that in times like this—called to look beyond this vale of tears to the place where God will wipe all tears from our eyes.

- He deepened our love.

The outpouring of love has been amazing. Total strangers have prayed for Mya to get well and wept for her passing—having never met her, they loved her. The Enka-Candler community has been reminded of the importance of love—loving your family, loving each other, and loving God. Have we not held our children and grandchildren just a little tighter since these events?

• He renewed our commitment.

It is not an exaggeration for me to tell you of scores of people who said they had strayed from God—had gotten cold and apathetic in their relationship with Him. Mya provided the spark that rekindled a flame in them.

• He brought souls to salvation.

One mother told me about her young son hearing of Mya's death and realizing that it could be him—and that he was not ready to meet Jesus. With weeping, he bowed his head and received Christ. There may be others reading these words that will make the same commitment—whether young or old. I am so thankful that, at Pole Creek's 2015 Vacation Bible School, Mya prayed to receive Christ and that spring of 2016, I baptized her—just months before her death.

• He summoned forth goodness in others.

There is so much evil in our world. You cannot turn on the TV without seeing the hate and the badness. We forget that there is also a lot of goodness—and Mya brought that out. People took time to pray, to make a blanket, to buy a stuffed animal, to fix a casserole, to send a card, to raise thousands of dollars—and on and on I could go.

- He reminded us of the value of time and the significance of living for eternity.

This sifted our priorities. Mya's story is a reminder of the brevity of life and gravity of eternity—and that much of what we think is important is actual trivial, and the spiritual and relational—family and church—are vital.

- He prepared for her an eternal weight of glory.

Paul tells us that the sufferings of this time serve a purpose—that they are preparing for us an eternal weight of glory—that heaven will be more enjoyable for the heartache we have endured here. Why would God have given Mya such gifts—so athletically inclined—if she would not be able to use them? She will! The Word of God declares, *"For the gifts and the calling of God are irrevocable"* (Romans 11:29).

Randy Alcorn wrote in his wonderful book simply entitled, "Heaven."

> Are you living with the disappointment of unfulfilled dreams? In heaven, you will find their fulfillment. Did poverty, poor health, war or lack of time prevent you from pursuing an adventure or dream? Did you never get to finish building that boat, or painting that picture, or writing that book—or reading that pile of books? Good news. On the New Earth you will have a second chance to do what you dreamed of doing—and far more besides . . . The

smartest person God ever created in this world may have never learned to read because he or she had no opportunity. The most musically gifted person may never have touched an instrument. The greatest athlete may never have competed in a game. The sport your best at may be a sport you have never tried, because your favorite hobby is one that you have thought of. The reversing of the Curse, and the resurrection of our bodies and our Earth, mean we will regain lost opportunities and inherit many more.[25]

As much as we will miss Mya, we would not call her back from that incredible place. Indeed, we cannot, but we can go to her. I am planning to see her again soon.

If life is really about giving God glory, then in seven years Mya has glorified her God. We may ask, "Would God not have been glorified more if she had risen and walked—giving her a long life?" Not necessarily.

I have a number of Bible commentaries by the late James Montgomery Boice, who pastored Tenth Presbyterian Church in Philadelphia for 32 years. He was diagnosed with liver cancer in May 2000. Here is what he said to his congregation:

> Should you pray for a miracle? Well, you're free to do that, of course. My general impression is that the God who is able to do miracles—and He certainly can—is also able to keep you from getting the problem in the first place. So, although miracles

---

[25] Alcorn, Randy. *Heaven* (Carol Stream, IL: Tyndale Momentum, 2004) 433-434

do happen, they're rare by definition.... Above all, I would say pray for the glory of God. If you think of God glorifying Himself in history and you say, where in all of history has God most glorified Himself? He did it at the cross of Jesus Christ, and it wasn't by delivering Jesus from the cross, though He could have....

God is in charge. When things like this come into our lives, they are not accidental. It's not as if God somehow forgot what was going on, and something bad slipped by.... God is not only the one who is in charge; God is also good. Everything He does is good.... If God does something in your life, would you change it? If you'd change it, you'd make it worse. It wouldn't be as good."[26]

A woman, Joni Eareckson Tada—herself no stranger to suffering, having been a quadriplegic since a diving accident in 1967–states it so profoundly, "God permits what He hates to accomplish that which He loves."[27]

The devil whispers in our ear the words of Job's wife, *"Curse God and die!"* (Job 2:9). Let us answer with Job, *"The Lord gave, and the Lord has taken away; Blessed be the name of the Lord"* (Job 1:21). Scripture tells us that Job lost almost everything—his wealth, his health, and suffered the death of all his children. At

---

[26] Alcorn, Randy. *If God Is Good: Faith in the Midst of Suffering and Evil* (:Multnomah, 2014), 14-15.

[27] Joni E. Tada and Steve Estes, *When God Weeps* (Grand Rapids: Zondervan, 1997), 84.

the end of the book, God restored double everything Job lost. You can read and calculate it—except in one case: Job had seven sons and three daughters who all died in a violent storm, so we would expect to read that in the end he had double—fourteen sons and six daughters. Yet, it says God gave him seven sons and three daughters! What? I thought God doubled all he lost; He did—something is not lost if you know where it is! Job knew his first set of children were in heaven! I still have at the time of writing, thirteen grandchildren! Twelve are here and one is in heaven.

CHAPTER 17

A GRIEF OBTAINED

→→→→ ❉ ←←←←

Years ago, the great Christian thinker, C.S. Lewis, wrote a book entitled *A Grief Observed*.[28] In this brief, but poignant volume, he describes his struggle after his wife dies. The pious platitudes and Christian clichés so often employed in the midst of sorrow were found to be hollow. Lewis wavered in maintaining a faith that had seemed so rock-solid. Once he spoke with such conviction about the things of God, as if he had all the answers. Suddenly, he was thrust into an abyss where answers could not be found.

The reality of a loved one's death to Lewis was brutal; the death of a loved one always is. Have you ever watched a seven-year old granddaughter who had been so full of life a year ago be consumed with cancer? Have you ever sat down with your son-in-law and your daughter to plan a funeral service that you will conduct? I hope not—and pray you never do! The pain is excruciating. I know that many of you who read this have been in similar times—a

---

[28] Lewis, Clive Staples. *A Grief Observed* (London: Faber and Faber, 1961).

A Grief Obtained

spouse, a sibling, a son—someone so dear and near and now all that remains are tombstones and memories.

I recall as a young pastor, visiting the hospital, seeking to minister by encouragement, Scripture, and prayer—and maybe somewhat effectively. Yet, it was theoretical. Nothing helped me be more helpful than when I was hospitalized for a week with a major operation, requiring a month to recuperate. My sympathy factor increased exponentially, and I believe my ministry was enhanced. No longer had theory, but experience, given me a platform of compassion.

I believe that is what Paul was saying in 2 Corinthians 1:3-7:

> *Blessed be the God and Father of our Lord Jesus Christ, the Father of mercies and God of all comfort, who comforts us in all our affliction, so that we may be able to comfort those who are in any affliction, with the comfort with which we ourselves are comforted by God. For as we share abundantly in Christ's sufferings, so through Christ we share abundantly in comfort too. If we are afflicted, it is for your comfort and salvation; and if we are comforted, it is for your comfort, which you experience when you patiently endure the same sufferings that we suffer. Our hope for you is unshaken, for we know that as you share in our sufferings, you will also share in our comfort.*[29]

---

[29] Crossway Bibles. *English Standard Version* (Wheaton, Ill: Crossway Bibles, 2007).

When Mya's Dad, Logan, asked me if I would preach Mya's funeral, I told him I could not. Nevertheless, I said that God would help me and if he wanted, I would try. It was both the hardest and easiest funeral I have ever done. Hardest because I am very weak; easiest because God is very strong.

I have no idea how many hundreds of funerals I have officiated and can truly say I have sought to weep with those that wept and bring them comfort. People have told me that they have been helped by my ministry in their bereavement. Yet, I know now what I have never known before. I have felt a heartache from which I will never recover until the great Resurrection Day. That hope seems more precious than ever to me! I can testify that God's grace is enough—that His comfort is real—and He will do the same for you, no matter what trial may come.

Kelly wrote her final post on CaringBridge:

> I have debated on posting one last time or not. Would it be some type of closure? I decided it would be, for CaringBridge. But not for Mya. There is no closure. There is no end. My baby is more alive than she has ever been. Healthier and happier than she has ever been. I am so thankful that is true for her. However, it is not true for me. I am sadder than I have ever been. I am hurting more than I ever have. In addition, it is a type of pain that cannot be described. I know there is hope. I will see her beautiful face again and my relationship with her will be even closer and better than what we had here. I look forward to that day! But knowing hope and

experiencing hope are not the same. Right now, I know in my head that hope is real. But my heart is struggling. The grief is strong. I am praying for the day that I feel God restoring that hope in my heart—that he will comfort me and give me peace. I do not want to live this life without her. Please pray for our family as we try to figure out how to continue when things are so different. God is the only one who can heal and I am trusting Him to do that.

And my prayer for anyone who has read these updates—is that you will truly know God. He is real. Jesus is real. Heaven is real. Hell is real. You will live forever, somewhere. There is no closure for you either. There is no end. There is no better way to honor our daughter's life and to encourage our family in this pain, than to know that someone made a commitment to follow Christ.

There will be justice
All will be new
Your name forever
Faithful and true
Jesus is coming soon.

Like a bride waiting for her groom.
We'll be a church, ready for you
Every heart longing for our King
We sing

Into The Valley of Shadow

> Even so come.
> Lord Jesus, come.[30]

Amen and amen.

---

[30] Jess Cates, Chris Tomlin, Jason Ingram. *Even So Come (Come Lord Jesus)*. (Worship Together Music, 2015)

Chapter 18

A Birthday Poem and Drawings in Chalk

—»»» ❊ «««—

O n her first birthday in heaven, I wrote a poem.

In honor of Mya's birthday:

Even though the pain is great,
we cannot help but celebrate
the day we all came face to face
with that beautiful little girl, Mya Grace.

Her precious smile could light up a room
and her little giggle could drive away any gloom.
Too soon, she left this place,
that beautiful little girl, Mya Grace.

Birthdays are supposed to be filled with cake, gifts, friends
and families.

> Nevertheless, today our family will gather to shed many tears and share fond memories.
>
> We take joy in knowing that our precious little one
> is safe in the arms of God's only Son.
> With that we know when we leave this place,
> we will see you again, our sweet Mya Grace.

A week later, Lyla wrote in chalk on my driveway:

> Bless the Lord, Oh my soul! I hope your [sic] having fun in haven [sic]. I love Mya!!! Miss you. Love Lyla!"

They were more like sisters, than cousins. Two peas in a pod. It was quite fitting that she wrote these words in chalk—symbolic of the fleeting nature of life. How quickly chalk fades away, and so does our life. Scripture calls it a vapor—a morning mist—that seems so substantial, only to dissipate before the sun as it climbs into the sky.

Chapter 19

WHY?

Why? It is the age-old question isn't it? Read the book of Job and see how that righteous man questioned God. Why is a persistent thread—for which he does not get a final answer. You can read the book of Job and gain insight on suffering. The gracious Lord allows us to see things unknown to his servant insofar as we are aware, but final solutions to this vexing matter of suffering and evil elude us and await eternity. By the end of the book, the focus shifts from why to Who—from Job and his groaning to God and His glory; no more the pain, but a Person that comes front and center. In the final analysis, even in ways we cannot comprehend, God is working all things for our good and His glory, accomplishing His purposes in methods we cannot fathom, but that will lead us on the other side to look back in awe—to fall at His feet and worship! Paul said this, *"For now we see in a mirror dimly, but then face to face. Now I know in part, but then I shall know just as I am known."* (1 Corinthians 13:12)

So, is it all right to ask God why? Surely—for Jesus did. Yet, there comes a point we may move beyond asking to anger, from painful perplexity to blasphemous bitterness. Job was edging that way, until God showed up and then this man had to shut up.

I cannot begin to tell you why my granddaughter had such a battle for her life—seven years old, and Mya was consumed with cancer. She had so much potential—a young flower just blooming and to be so soon wilted and perishing under a searing sun of suffering—why?

Please, do not suggest your reasons. Do not become Job's friends. Silent sympathy is far better than incomplete instruction that contains a hint of accusation—something that should not be in your life (sin) or a lack of something in your life (faith). Indeed, I should have less sin and more faith—and am seeking forgiveness and faith from the Lord.

Instead, let me leave it at the feet of Jesus in worship—commit it into the Father's good hands as Jesus did with His last breath on the cross, and submit to Him as Job ultimately would.

Then, there is this—I was contacted by a mother who told me her young son became convicted of sin, alarmed at the prospect of his own death upon hearing about Mya. He prayed to receive Christ! Jesus said that the value of a soul was worth more than the whole world and heaven celebrates each lost one being found! Other stories of Mya's impact on lives are increasing by the day. Therefore, we are finding reasons to rejoice in this trial. God is up to something. On the other side, we will see it clearly. For now, we cling to faith, hope, and love.

Recently, someone began a discussion of this topic by stating, "If I was God" and then proceeded to say how they would run the

WHY?

universe. I answered that by humbly stating that I am not God and do not have all the answers. I went on to say:

> Let me begin with your statement, "If I was God." That is the problem. It is why we have suffering. Satan offered humanity the temptation, "Eat this fruit and you'll be as God." Adam and Eve ate, and sin entered the world along with all the horror that accompanies it.
>
> Things are broken and God will fix them. We may be sure that infinite intelligence and perfect love is working out all for His glory and the ultimate good.
>
> God gave us freedom to love Him or reject Him. Sadly, most choose the latter. It was never God's original plan for there to be death and suffering.
>
> Jesus said that God sees even a sparrow when it falls to the ground and He cares. Therefore, we know He cares for little children. He suffers and grieves with us and for us.

Some suffering is a direct result of personal sin—either our own, or evil done to us because of the sinful choice of others. If I drink and destroy my liver, the suffering is from my sin. If I am injured from being hit by a drunk driver, I suffer from their sin. Sinful choices bring consequences—there is a cause and effect relationship.

It is particularly hard to deal with the pictures of suffering of little children, hungry and starving in third world countries. It is not from lack of resources, but sin—selfishness and false religion.

I have been to India, where there is still grinding poverty. While people are begging for a morsel, or scavenging garbage for scraps, sacred cows wander around. India produces enough grain to feed its populace, but rats consume a lot of that grain. You cannot kill them. It might be Grandma or Uncle Joe reincarnated!

Then, there is the sin of the church that is meant to be the extension of Christ's love to the world. We throw away enough food and eat more than we ought, which could be used to feed these starving children. The sin of covetousness is routinely practiced among those who claim to be followers of Jesus.

Furthermore, if false religion proliferates and people suffer from its effects, we must ask how much we are investing in sharing the Gospel. Too often, we waste money on trivial trinkets that could have been used supporting missions. Have we even considered that God might want us to step out of the comfort of our consumer mentality and go into the world with the Word? Therefore, we must not blame an apathetic God who is anything but that. He has given us a plan and the provision. We own the apathy!

Some suffering is divine discipline—which is not necessarily punitive, but formative—meant to shape us into the image of Christ. One ought to study Romans 8 intensively. A couple of verses are at the core of this vexing problem of suffering and God's involvement or seeming lack thereof:

> *And we know that all things work together for good to those who love God, to those who are the called*

according to His purpose. For whom He foreknew, He also predestined to be conformed to the image of His Son, that He might be the firstborn among many brethren. (Romans 8:28-29)

Far from this being a sign of God's spite, it is the assurance of His love. Hebrews 12 gives us the classic call to look to a suffering Savior for the example of endurance. We are reminded where there is no pain, there is no gain. This is not only true in the realm of sports, but in the sphere of the spiritual. Discipline, although painful, serves a purpose.

Therefore we also, since we are surrounded by so great a cloud of witnesses, let us lay aside every weight, and the sin which so easily ensnares us, and let us run with endurance the race that is set before us, looking unto Jesus, the author and finisher of our faith, who for the joy that was set before Him endured the cross, despising the shame, and has sat down at the right hand of the throne of God. For consider Him who endured such hostility from sinners against Himself, lest you become weary and discouraged in your souls. You have not yet resisted to bloodshed, striving against sin. And you have forgotten the exhortation which speaks to you as to sons: "My son, do not despise the chastening of the LORD, Nor be discouraged when you are rebuked by Him; For whom the LORD loves He chastens, And scourges every son whom He receives." If you

> *endure chastening, God deals with you as with sons; for what son is there whom a father does not chasten? But if you are without chastening, of which all have become partakers, then you are illegitimate and not sons. Furthermore, we have had human fathers who corrected us, and we paid them respect. Shall we not much more readily be in subjection to the Father of spirits and live? For they indeed for a few days chastened us as seemed best to them, but He for our profit, that we may be partakers of His holiness. Now no chastening seems to be joyful for the present, but painful; nevertheless, afterward it yields the peaceable fruit of righteousness to those who have been trained by it.* (Hebrews 12:1-11)

James, half-brother of our Lord Jesus, writes in his letter to a group of Jewish believers scattered abroad by persecution. He encourages them to not only endure the suffering, but also enjoy the result:

> *My brethren, count it all joy when you fall into various trials, knowing that the testing of your faith produces patience. But let patience have its perfect work, that you may be perfect and complete, lacking nothing.* (James 1:2-4)

The trial itself is not the joyful part. We are not called to be spiritual masochists! If God did not want us free from pain, He would have us "enjoy" that for all eternity! The fact is that we will rejoice in God's work through thrusting us into the fire and hammering us on the anvil to temper our faith when we get to glory.

The songwriter said it well:

"It Will Be Worth It All"
>Sometimes the day seems long,
>Our trials hard to bear.
>We're tempted to complain,
>to murmur and despair.
>But Christ will soon appear
>to catch his bride away!
>All tears forever over
>in God's eternal day!
>
>At times the sky seems dark,
>with not a ray of light;
>We're tossed and driven on,
>no human help in sight.
>But there is One in heaven,
>Who knows our deepest care;
>Let Jesus solve your problems,
>just go to him in prayer.
>
>Life's day will soon be o're,
>all storms forever past;
>We'll cross the great divide
>to Glory, safe at last!
>We'll share the joys of heaven:
>a harp, a home, a crown;

The tempter will be banished,
We'll lay our burdens down.

CHORUS:
It will be worth it all
when we see Jesus!
Life's trials will seem so small
when we see Christ.
One glimpse of his dear face,
all sorrow will erase.
So, bravely run the race
till we see Christ.[31]

The Apostle Paul—a great sufferer and a godly saint—spoke to this in 2 Corinthians 4:16-18.

Therefore we do not lose heart. Even though our outward man is perishing, yet the inward man is being renewed day by day. For our light affliction, which is but for a moment, is working for us a far more exceeding and eternal weight of glory, while we do not look at the things which are seen, but at the things which are not seen. For the things which are seen are temporary, but the things which are not seen are eternal.

---

[31] Rusthoi, Esther *It Will Be Worth It All* (Brentwood-Benson Music Publishing, Inc. 1941)

WHY?

We are reminded that there are things we do not know. To look around at the circumstance is to see only from a materialistic view and find little meaning in our mess. To see with eyes of faith the invisible, spiritual dimension is to discover God's glorious intent for light, momentary affliction. That is, God limits the scope and span of suffering to that which will not truly harm us (only our body which in its present state is incapable of dwelling in heaven anyway) but will actually help us to become more like Jesus!

The stories of two Old Testament characters give us a peek behind the veil into the sometimes-mystifying ways of God.

The aforementioned Job presents to us this struggle of coming to grips with why God allows suffering, and although not giving us all the answers, manifesting to us a Sovereign God who is all we need in the midst of our heartache. We do not know if Job ever understood the clash of forces in the heavenly realm because of God's challenge to Satan that would transform Job's life into the battlefield, but we know by the inspiration of the Holy Spirit, and can be helped through knowing that we too choose this:

> *Then Job arose, tore his robe, and shaved his head; and he fell to the ground and worshiped. And he said: "Naked I came from my mother's womb, And naked shall I return there. The LORD gave, and the LORD has taken away; Blessed be the name of the LORD." In all this Job did not sin nor charge God with wrong.* (Job 1:20-22)

Joseph's story brings us another angle. In summary, Genesis 37-50 recounts a man who was faithful to God, and yet it seemed

God was not faithful to him. He tried to follow a God-given dream and each step took him into deeper misery. From the pit of slavery and deeper into the prison of abandonment; hated by his brothers, slandered by his employer's wife, forgotten by a man he befriended—for two years—and God was where? Engineering all things to elevate Joseph eventually to prominence in Egypt where he would be used to save his family and see God keep His covenant promise. Think about this: if there had been no Joseph in his suffering, there would be no Jesus with His salvation!

Several times Joseph acknowledges the unseen hand of God orchestrating events—even evil ones—for good. *"But as for you, you meant evil against me; but God meant it for good, in order to bring it about as it is this day, to save many people alive."* (Genesis 50:20)

If you want to argue with Paul about the amount of pain you are going through and claim it to be anything but light and momentary, consider it is a relative term in comparison to the weight and length of eternity. Neither was Paul sitting in an ivory tower insulated from hurt and writing mere theories. Here is a summary of his sufferings:

> *Are they ministers of Christ?—I speak as a fool—I am more: in labors more abundant, in stripes above measure, in prisons more frequently, in deaths often. From the Jews five times I received forty stripes minus one. Three times I was beaten with rods; once I was stoned; three times I was shipwrecked; a night and a day I have been in the deep; in journeys often, in perils of waters, in perils of robbers, in perils*

of my own countrymen, in perils of the Gentiles, in perils in the city, in perils in the wilderness, in perils in the sea, in perils among false brethren; in weariness and toil, in sleeplessness often, in hunger and thirst, in fastings often, in cold and nakedness—besides the other things, what comes upon me daily: my deep concern for all the churches. Who is weak, and I am not weak? Who is made to stumble, and I do not burn with indignation? If I must boast, I will boast in the things which concern my infirmity. The God and Father of our Lord Jesus Christ, who is blessed forever, knows that I am not lying. In Damascus the governor, under Aretas the king, was guarding the city of the Damascenes with a garrison, desiring to arrest me; but I was let down in a basket through a window in the wall, and escaped from his hands. (2 Corinthians 11:23-33)

While I would not minimize the pain that anyone goes through, not many of us would claim to be on the level of intense suffering as the Apostle.

He was not Superman! He was a real man of flesh and blood, and who sought to be delivered from pain if possible. That is our instinctive reaction—God-given for preservation! Was Jesus wrong to pray in Gethsemane that the horror of the cross might be avoided if possible? No! Not when He went on to submit Himself to the Father's will. We hear this echoed in Paul:

It is doubtless not profitable for me to boast. I will come to visions and revelations of the Lord: I know a man in Christ who fourteen years ago—whether in the body I do not know, or whether out of the body I do not know, God knows—such a one was caught up to the third heaven. And I know such a man—whether in the body or out of the body I do not know, God knows—how he was caught up into Paradise and heard inexpressible words, which it is not lawful for a man to utter. Of such a one I will boast; yet of myself I will not boast, except in my infirmities. For though I might desire to boast, I will not be a fool; for I will speak the truth. But I refrain, lest anyone should think of me above what he sees me to be or hears from me. And lest I should be exalted above measure by the abundance of the revelations, a thorn in the flesh was given to me, a messenger of Satan to buffet me, lest I be exalted above measure. Concerning this thing I pleaded with the Lord three times that it might depart from me. And He said to me, "My grace is sufficient for you, for My strength is made perfect in weakness." Therefore most gladly I will rather boast in my infirmities, that the power of Christ may rest upon me. Therefore I take pleasure in infirmities, in reproaches, in needs, in persecutions, in distresses, for Christ's sake. For when I am weak, then I am strong. (2 Corinthians 12:1-10)

WHY?

Another question I was asked is connected to this, "Why does it seem that the people, who serve God, suffer the most?"

The reality is this is apparently true. Living in a fallen world means none are exempt from pain. The rain falls on the just and the unjust. Storms come to those who build on the Rock of Ages and those who build on the sands of time.

Perhaps those who choose to enjoy the pleasures of sin for a season are allowed by a gracious God to have a taste of goodness since they will suffer forever in hell eventually. That very goodness of God is meant to capture their attention, *"Or do you despise the riches of His goodness, forbearance, and longsuffering, not knowing that the goodness of God leads you to repentance?"* (Romans 2:4)

We may also say that whatever pain we go through as God's children is only for this world. There is no purgatory after death, but there is one before it—and that is this planet of pain. Here is the truth according to Jesus, *"These things I have spoken to you, that in Me you may have peace. In the world you will have tribulation; but be of good cheer, I have overcome the world."* (John 16:33)

Suffering, as all things, will eventually redound to God's glory.

The ninth chapter of John's Gospel points this out:

> *Now as Jesus passed by, He saw a man who was blind from birth. And His disciples asked Him, saying, "Rabbi, who sinned, this man or his parents, that he was born blind?" Jesus answered, "Neither this man nor his parents sinned, but that the works of God should be revealed in him.* (John 9:1-3)

The disciples had bought into the erroneous doctrine that all suffering is the direct result of one's personal sin. In this case, it would be the prenatal sin of the man or some evil of his parents that caused him to be born blind. This was the false ideology Job's "friends" had when they accused him of suffering because of his sinful acts. The book of Job refuted that, but apparently, the disciples had not studied that, as they should.

From eternity, an omniscient God knew that one day a baby would be born blind. That child would go through years of growing up in darkness—and despair. However, this omnipotent God was also planning to send His Son to exhibit that power. The result would be the man's good and God's glory. All things are moving inexorably toward His glory and not all Satan does can stop it.

I heard the late Dr. Bruce Dunn tell this story in a sermon years ago at Ben Lippen Bible Conference. Please overlook the term used to describe a child with Down's syndrome. It is not a politically correct term, but was a common expression for the times. The message is insightful, nevertheless.

> I would like to share with you a true story, which has made a great impact on me and truly touched my heart. A special week of meetings were being held by a guest speaker, Dr. Donald Barnhouse. During the course of the week, the pastor's wife gave birth to a mongoloid baby. Both the pastor and his wife were grievous and wondered how to cope with the situation. Dr. Barnhouse shared with them a portion of Scripture in Exodus 4, where God seemed to have taken upon Himself the complete

responsibility for human suffering. Moses had stubbornly refused to accept God's call because of inadequacy and the Lord's reply was, *"...who maketh the dumb, or deaf, or the seeing, or the blind? Have not I, the Lord?"* (Exodus 4:11).

Through prayer and tears with one another, the pastor and his wife were able to say, "God has blessed us with a mongoloid baby."

The next step was for the pastor's wife to call her family and share with them their recent experience. There was a switchboard operator in the hospital who 'had it in' for Christians and couldn't stand them. With a cynical attitude, she processed the call and listened in on the conversation. She was appalled at what she heard and immediately spread the word to the rest of the hospital personnel.

The following Sunday morning the pastor stood to preach and in closing he gave an invitation for people to come forward. He bowed his head in prayer and didn't look around. There were several dozen or more of the hospital staff in the service that morning and when he gave the invitation, a couple dozen of them were standing down at the front of the altar asking Jesus Christ to be their Savior.

Into The Valley of Shadow

That mongoloid baby grew to about 15 years of age and then went home to Heaven. Some years later, a woman called the pastor expressing a real need for his help. She explained that she was the wife of the doctor who had brought his mongoloid baby into the world. She proceeded to explain that at this moment her husband was locked in his room with a revolver in his hands ready to kill himself. The doctor had told his wife that the only person he was willing to talk to would be this pastor. The pastor immediately went to his home and asked for his gun and talked to him about Christ. The doctor gave the gun to the pastor and also received Christ as his Savior at that time!

The pastor and his wife knew that God was involved in their lives! They were willing to say that it isn't all sweet roses and perfume, but God is involved and they were not going to rebel and be bitter, but they were going to say, "Lord, we can't figure things out and we don't like it, but Thy will be done." Then peace came and as a result many people came to Jesus.[32]

Now, I have written a much longer chapter than most of the others in this book, but have only scratched the surface of this perplexing matter. Volumes have been written by some of far greater

---

[32] (http://www.biblicalevangelist.org/index.php?view=Sermons&id=797&issue=Volume+32,+Number+4)

intellect than I have, so I have no illusions as to give you all the answers. I hope I have given you something to chew on to nourish your faith.

Even so, we must acknowledge with Paul,

> *Oh, the depth of the riches both of the wisdom and knowledge of God! How unsearchable are His judgments and His ways past finding out! "For who has known the mind of the LORD? Or who has become His counselor?" "Or who has first given to Him And it shall be repaid to him?" For of Him and through Him and to Him are all things, to whom be glory forever. Amen.* (Romans 11:33-36)

Amen!

Chapter 20

More Memories

Strange how memory works—the things that just hit you unexpectedly. When Mya was hospitalized so long for cancer treatment, one of the things she loved for me to bring her was a vanilla bean Frappuccino from Starbucks. She thought it tasted like snow cream. How much I would love to buy her a frappe again! Oh well, she is eating manna from the Master's table and drinking from the crystal-clear river of life that flows from the throne of God!

On July 14, 2017, my eldest, Chris, posted this on Facebook:

> One year ago, today, I sat in a hospital agonizing over the fact that at any moment my niece would draw her last breath this side of Heaven. How could this be happening? She was supposed to be out running around in the yard, playing with her siblings, giggling with the joy of being young and carefree.

More Memories

In the weeks leading up to this moment I had felt strongly that God would intervene and spare her life. Songs that seem to come on the radio all the time encouraged me that God was moving and that we just needed to keep the faith. Twice in one day, I saw the same passage of Scripture in Matthew 19 referencing Jesus's words that all things were possible with God. Surely, it must be a sign of my little niece walking out of that hospital and back into life.

Yet, here we were. Sitting in this room full of tears, praying for a miracle and yet knowing deep down that this was going to be the night that Mya went home to be with her Savior. As I sat in that room, many questions flooded my mind:

- How was my baby sister going to survive losing her baby girl?

- How was my brother-in-law going to stay strong for his family while hurting so much for his little girl?

- How would my sister's other children cope with the loss of their sister?

- How were my parents going to survive all of the stress that they had been dealing with at home while also experiencing the loss of my Dad's father and their grandchild?

- How were my sister's in-laws going to deal with the tragic loss of a second grandchild while also having dealt with the loss of their middle son in the prime of his life?

- How was I going to explain to my children that their cousin was not going to be around to grow old with them?

It was just in the past couple of days, as I reflected on these events, that I realized what God was trying to tell me in those days leading up to her death. The answer to all of the questions listed above was so simple, yet so profound - *"But with God all things are possible."* (Matthew 19:6)

What is possible with God? Everything! How could a sinful man like me be counted as a child of God? How could the sin that brought this dreaded disease into this world be overcome? How can a person have peace in the midst of immense suffering? *"But with God all things are possible."*

My prayer today is for each of you to place your faith in the One who made all things possible. The Bible says that you only need to *"confess with your mouth the Lord Jesus and believe in your heart that God raised Him from the dead, you will be saved"*. (Romans 10:9)

How hard are the holidays still! Filled with memories and the conscious absence of sweet Mya Grace.

There is Thanksgiving without Mya at our table—yet she is everywhere: her pictures on the wall, her name on our lips, her sweet face engraved in our memory, and the afterglow of her presence sparkling in the tear that runs down the channel in my face and lands in the corner of a smile. We will always miss you at our table, Mya, but what a feast you are enjoying! Save a place for me. We will eat together again someday!

I recall as Marilyn and I watched videos of Mya's last Christmas at home last evening and the next day was given a book from Logan and Kelly, in which Mya's mom photographed such precious pictures.

My reaction surprised me. As I watched her face beam and eyes sparkle in opening her presents, listened to her laugh and express such gratitude to her Dad and Mom, and saw these pictures of her among the flowers and sunshine, hugging up on her siblings, and watching with wonder as a caterpillar crawled up her skin, I wept much.

That was not surprising. I have been doing a lot of that. These tears certainly were an expression of sorrow—but more. They were hot tears of anger. I am angry with a child fighting so hard and being subjected to so much—of months confined in a hospital room battling cancer—to no avail. I am angry at hopes dashed. It is a slow, simmering fury that lurks under the surface. I want to scream. I confess that as I have driven by her grave going home that I have at times smashed my fist into the dashboard.

To think that Mya cannot be with us to open Christmas presents and play with her cousins—to dress up and be part of the kids' nativity reenactment—is painful. I watch her parents' struggle. My little girl Kelly, ought to be standing beside Mya in front of a Christmas tree, full of joy, instead of broken-hearted in front of a tombstone.

I am angry about it all.

You may say I should not feel that way. It may bother you to hear a preacher speak that way. Understand, I am not mad at God. I resist all temptations to curse Him and with Job say, *"The LORD gave, and the, and the LORD has taken away; Blessed be the name of the Lord."* (Job 1:21b) Yet, I say it in faith resting in what I know in my head. How I feel in my heart at this moment is another matter.

I am angry at sickness, cancer, death—the curse on this sinful world in which we live. I feel as though I have been robbed. Could I exchange places today, I would—a sweet girl playing as my family remembers me and looks forward to seeing me again in heaven.

We cling to hope. I will see Mya in a better place with no more tears—but today, there are bitter tears of anger and disappointment.

Then, there was this—I went to the hospital to visit a child in pediatric ICU. It did not dawn on me until I got to the hospital that I had not been back in that area since Mya's death. It was very surreal. Therefore, on her birthday, I spent some time in that room which seemed far too familiar. Though we miss her, I am glad she can now run down the golden streets of glory without an IV pole attached!

> Mya, I will see you later!

> Bless the Lord oh my soul
> Oh my soul

Worship His Holy name
Sing like never before
Oh my soul
I'll worship Your Holy name

The sun comes up
It's a new day dawning
It's time to sing Your song again
Whatever may pass
And whatever lies before me
Let me be singing
When the evening comes

Bless the Lord oh my soul
Oh my soul
Worship His Holy name
Sing like never before
Oh my soul
I'll worship Your Holy name

You're rich in love
And You're slow to anger
Your name is great
And Your heart is kind
For all Your goodness
I will keep on singing
Ten thousand reasons
For my heart to find

Bless the Lord oh my soul
Oh my soul
Worship His Holy name
Sing like never before
Oh my soul
I'll worship Your Holy name

And on that day
When my strength is failing
The end draws near
And my time has come
Still my soul will
Sing Your praise unending
Ten thousand years
And then forevermore
Forevermore

Bless the Lord oh my soul
Oh my soul
Worship His Holy name
Sing like never before
Oh my soul
I'll worship Your Holy name

Bless the Lord oh my soul
Oh my soul
Worship His Holy name
Sing like never before
Oh my soul

More Memories

I'll worship Your Holy name
Yes I'll worship Your Holy name
Lord I'll worship Your Holy name[33]

---

[33] Lyrics.com, STANDS4 LLC, 2019. "10,000 Reasons (Bless the Lord) Lyrics." Accessed August 5, 2019. https://www.lyrics.com/lyric/35345919/Matt+Redman.

Conclusion

From Mya's Mother Kelly:
Moving Forward

Waking up to a new sunrise
Looking back from the other side
I can see now with open eyes
Darkest water and deepest pain
I wouldn't trade it for anything
'cause my brokenness brought me to You
And these wounds are a story You'll use
So I'm thankful for the scars
'cause without them I wouldn't know your heart
And I know they'll always tell of who You are
So forever I am thankful for the scars"[34]

—I Am They

---

[34] Ethan Hulse, Jon McConnell, Matthew Armstrong, Matthew Hein. *Scars* (Warner Chappell Music, Inc. 2018)

Into The Valley of Shadow

These are some of the lyrics to a song that means so much to me. I think about how scars are the sign of healing. On this earth, my wounds are open and raw, but I am holding onto the promise that one day God will wipe away every tear. Then, I will be totally healed. I am not thankful for what has happened to our family, but I am thankful that God carries us and reminds me of his love, and for the scars he promises are to come.

As I write this, we are approaching what would have been Mya's 10th birthday. It is hard to believe in so many ways. At one moment, it can feel like she was just here and the very next moment I feel like I have not seen her in 100 years. My arms literally ache to hold her. Time has a strange way of playing with your emotions. I know some people say time heals, but I cannot completely agree with that. Is time healing our hurt? Has it helped with the immense pain that our family felt on that horrible day in 2016? The short answer is no. Some of the grief fog has lifted, but there is no amount of time that can heal a hurt this deep. Our only healing will be Heaven. However, God has given us time as a gift. It has made us aware of how frail life is, and how quickly it is vanishing. We are trying to use our time wisely and make our lives count for Christ while we are waiting (sometimes impatiently) until the day we are with Him in Heaven.

Logan and I were at dinner one night when someone asked us how we were doing. In the words of my sweet and wise husband, "We are moving forward." I sat there, blinded by my tears, and realized that is the perfect description for our family. There is no moving on without our sweet girl—but we are moving forward. Our lives are still a daily struggle and I suspect that will never change—but, we are moving forward—with every day, every single breath, we are moving closer to seeing Mya and our family will never be separated again! From the depths of my heart, I pray even so come, Lord Jesus come!

Our prayer for you is that you can say those same words because you have the assurance of an eternity with Jesus!

Sincerely,
Kelly Phillips

CPSIA information can be obtained
at www.ICGtesting.com
Printed in the USA
BVHW051710231219
567575BV00019B/769/P